Paul Shaffer: *We'll Be Here for the Rest of Our Lives*
Grandmaster Flash: *My Life, My Beats*
Tavis Smiley: *What I Know for Sure*
Cornel West: *Brother West*
Archbishop Carl Bean: *I Was Born This Way*
Natalie Cole: *Love Brought Me Back*
Janet Jackson: *True You*
Scott Weiland: *Not Dead and Not for Sale*

NOVELS

Search for Happiness
The Man Who Brought the Dodgers Back to Brooklyn
Blues Notes Under a Green Felt Hat
Barbells and Saxophones
Family Blood
Take It Off! Take It All Off!
Passion Flowers
Sanctified Blues (cowritten with Mable John)
Stay Out of the Kitchen (cowritten with Mable John)
Love Tornado (cowritten with Mable John)
Power and Beauty (cowritten with Clifford "T.I." Harris Jr.)

INSPIRATIONAL

Messengers: Portraits of African American Ministers, Evangelists, Gospel Singers, and Other Messengers of "the Word"

A Moment in Time

AN AMERICAN STORY OF BASEBALL,
HEARTBREAK, AND GRACE

Ralph Branca

with David Ritz

SCRIBNER

New York London Toronto Sydney New Delhi

🔥 Scribner •
A Division of Simon & Schuster,
Inc. • 1230 Avenue of the Americas • New
York, NY 10020 • Copyright © 2011 by Ralph Branca and
David Ritz • All rights reserved, including the right to reproduce this
book or portions thereof in any form whatsoever. For information address
Scribner Subsidiary Rights Department, 1230 Avenue of the Americas,
New York, NY 10020. • First Scribner hardcover edition October 2011
• SCRIBNER and design are registered trademarks of The Gale Group,
Inc., used under license by Simon & Schuster, Inc., the publisher of this
work. • For information about special discounts for bulk purchases, please
contact Simon & Schuster Special Sales at 1-866-506-1949 or business
@simonandschuster.com. • The Simon & Schuster Speakers Bureau can
bring authors to your live event. For more information or to book an event
contact the Simon & Schuster Speakers Bureau at 1-866-248-3049 or visit
our website at www.simonspeakers.com. • Manufactured in the United
States of America • Library of Congress Control Number: 2011019549
• ISBN 978-1-4516-3690-1 •
(ebook) 10 9 8 7 6 5 4 3 2 1 •
• The Brooklyn Dodgers Rule! •

For my wife, Ann,
and my daughters, Patti and Mary

Contents

Contents

A Moment in Time

Introduction

I LOVE BASEBALL.

Baseball is the reason I am writing this book, the reason I've led a life worth reexamining and dissecting. Baseball is the passion that carried me from childhood to manhood. It is how I fought my way from the working class to the middle class. Were it not for baseball, I would not have met Ann, my wife, the mother of our daughters, and my dearest friend for the past sixty years. Baseball has excited my mind, stirred my soul, and brought out the best in me. I look at baseball deeply. Most of us whose lives have been defined by baseball do. Of course, it's principally a sport—a beautiful sport based on a poetic geometry. It is a game played outside of time. You play it not until the clock runs out, but until there is a clear winner. That takes as long as it takes. It is a pastoral game usually set inside a city. You play in a pasture—an urban pasture—where an expanse of grass calls you to the competition. Of course, you can also play on the dirt field of a farm, a sandlot, or a concrete street. Wherever you play, though, time is suspended. Like millions of other kids, I lost track of time whenever I played—playing through breakfast, lunch, dinner; playing until the very last rays of daylight disappeared; playing under the glow of a street lamp or a full moon; playing with the hope that

1

the game would never stop and that real time—any time but base-ball time—would never resume. The dream was to turn life into a baseball game.

Over time, as that dream came true, I saw other dimensions of the sport. It was a proving ground where character was developed or destroyed, enhanced or corroded. It was where racial animus was resolved or exacerbated. Because I was privileged to play when society was undergoing radical change, I got to see firsthand—from the dugout and the mound—baseball's reaction, for better and worse. I got to see—and feel and embrace—community. The Brooklyn baseball community was like no other; Brooklyn Dodger fans were the most knowledgeable. The Brooklyn ballpark was like no other. These were things I loved with all my heart: this proving ground, this social transformation, this extraordinary community.

The bigger story, then, speaks to the spirit of our country and our sense of the possible. It is about optimism, hope, and fairness. The smaller story—my personal story—benefits from those strong American values but also involves tremendous frustration and unforeseen corruption. The drama of ongoing disappointment is central to this narrative. At some point, reason and rage clashed head-on. For years, I struggled with anger and resentment.

This book represents the resolution of that resentment and the dissolution of the rage. To be called a goat—as I was—for more than half a century hurt like hell, especially when I knew that the team who tagged me with that label had implemented an elaborate and outrageous system of cheating. I had learned about the cheating less than three years after it happened. Yet for many long decades I kept quiet. I was advised to capitalize on and expose the scheme. Go to the press. Write a book. Do something. But I refused. I didn't want to be seen as a whiner, a sore loser, or a baby crying over spilt milk. Take it on the chin. Accept the blow. Move on with your life. Or, best of all, forget about it, which proved impossible.

Introduction

Bobby Thomson's home run off me in the 1951 playoff was termed "the shot heard 'round the world" and called the most dramatic moment in sports history. If it was shown once on television, it was shown a million times. No one could forget what had happened that afternoon in the Polo Grounds—not me, not the country, not history itself. I had to endure the moment in silence. I saw silence as my shield of dignity. I wanted to shout "Fraud!" but my nature wouldn't allow it.

Then, on January 31, 2001, journalist Joshua Prager broke the scandal in the *Wall Street Journal* and five years later published an exhaustively researched book scrupulously documenting the cheating. After the initial article came out, Bobby Thomson, by then my friend of many years, called and said, "I guess you feel exonerated, Ralph."

"I don't know about that," I replied, "but my tongue has certainly been loosened."

I'm grateful for that loosening. And I'm also glad that the loosening comes when, instead of still toiling in my mid-twenties, I'm reflecting in my mid-eighties. Time not only heals, but time also offers perspective. Seen through the misty glow of history, a story from a distant era takes on a romantic tinge. And the era of New York baseball of the forties and fifties when three winning teams—the Dodgers, Yankees, and Giants—dominated the headlines may be the most exciting years in all baseball. Looking back 60-plus years to a time when players—myself included—took the bus and subway to the ballpark and worked menial winter jobs to support our families, I can't quite believe the remarkable changes I've seen in this long lifetime. I cherish those changes just as I cherish that sacred time when, as a boy and young man, I never could have imagined baseball—or, for that matter, the world—in its present form. There's also an essential fact that, modesty aside, I want this book to establish: I was a damn effective pitcher. It pains me to be remembered for one unfortunate pitch—and, unfairly, a pitch surreptitiously signaled to the hitter—as opposed to a hurler who, for a number of years, had good stuff.

Finally, I must warn you that I write from the point of view of a self-proclaimed old-timer. I make no apologies for that designation. I love being an old-timer. Hell, I may be the ultimate old-timer. I feel like I've seen it all and done it all. I can truthfully say that I've paid the dues to tell the news. And even though I will try to recapture the fire and energy that at one time burned within the heart of an 18-year-old rookie breaking into the majors, be aware that this is a highly opinionated old-timer—who's about to spin a baseball yarn unlike any you've ever heard.

Ladies' Day

THE POLO GROUNDS was heaven.

My 10-year-old mind was not concerned with how the Depression was crippling the country, but only the happy fact that we—my mom, sisters, and brothers—were sitting in the upper-deck left-field stands watching the Giants play a doubleheader with the Cards. Only two years before, St. Louis had won the Series with its scrappy "Gashouse Gang" featuring Pepper Martin, Spud Davis, Frankie Frisch, and Leo Durocher. This year we'd get to see our Giants capture the pennant, only to lose the World Series to the Yanks.

On this day in September, we took a bus to the Eighth Avenue subway to reach the Polo Grounds. It was a quick and easy trip. The cloudless sky was blazing blue and the late summer sun comforting and warm. The air was clean. The prosciutto, provolone, and salami sandwiches made by Mom were spicy and delicious.

The year 1936 was a good one for baseball. A 21-year-old rookie named Joe DiMaggio was tearing up the American League. We called him Joe D and, as Italian Americans, were especially proud of his brilliant play. He'd wind up hitting .323 and smacking 29 home runs, nearly overshadowing the great Lou Gehrig who, at 33, hit .354 and belted 49 homers. Amazing things happened at Yankee Stadium.

That stadium also was part of our world—only 45 minutes from our house in Mount Vernon, just over the Bronx line. In the years that my baseball consciousness grew by leaps and bounds, the Yankees were the dominant force in the game. They won the World Series four straight times, from '36 through '39. But they were not my team. The Giants were. The Polo Grounds was my ballpark. It was a strange-shaped monster that looked like a bathtub. Coogan's Bluff, a hill that housed a line of apartment buildings, loomed over the home plate stands. The Harlem River rolled directly to the east. An enormous Chesterfield sign, with a gleaming white cigarette big enough for King Kong, sat in center field. Inside a swirl of smoke were the words "A HIT!" The "H" in "Chesterfield" would light up for a hit and the "E" for an error. Below the huge advertisement were the clubhouses and dead center field. No one in the history of the Polo Grounds had ever hit a ball to its outer limits, 475 feet from home plate. The dimensions of the park were always shrouded in mystery. It is my firm belief, by the way, that the distance to the right field foul pole was only 243 feet, not quite conforming to the rules of major league baseball requiring a minimum of 250 feet. Throughout my life, I'd hear different figures from different people. To a 10-year-old, the place was absolute grandeur. The men sanctioned to compete in this arena had the austerity and stature of gladiators. They were my heroes.

One of the first to capture my awe was Giant Mel Ott, the gutsy outfielder who batted left-handed but threw right, the youngest player to hit 100 home runs and the first National Leaguer to reach 500 homers, and to knock in more than 100 runs eight years in a row. Standing at the plate, he was so intimidating—even at only five-feet-nine—that he drew five walks in a single game three separate times. I loved to watch Mel lift his right forward foot a split second, then plant it before his bat met the ball, an ominous move.

My early heroes also included two brilliant Giant pitchers, Carl Hubbell and Hal Schumacher. On this day at the Polo Grounds, a third, Freddie Fitzsimmons, was facing the Cards in the first game of a doubleheader. We won 8–4. In the second game, St. Louis won 4–3, but I got to see two of their aces, Dizzy Dean and Roy Parmelee. I couldn't have been more thrilled; they were among the top pitchers in the game. My life was already about pitching because my big brother Jules—we called him Pops because he was 16 years older than me—would sit in a chair and make me throw at him. If the ball didn't land in his glove, I'd have to chase after it. I'd been trained that way since I was six. Two of my younger brothers, Paul and Al, were pitchers, and so was John, who was 18 months older. We were a baseball-crazed family.

In all, Mom had 17 children. Born Ralph (after my grandfather Raffaelo) Theodore (after Teddy Roosevelt) Branca, on January 6, 1926, I was sibling number 15. Mom's first two infants died of diphtheria. When I was 15 months, my 10-year-old sister Sylvia died of rheumatic fever. When I was 13, my sister Suzanne, then 16, died of pancreatic cancer. She was a beautiful young woman with great artistic talent. Her death became the great tragedy of my childhood. After that, I grew up with 12 siblings: sisters Florence, Helen, Margaret, Rosemary, Antoinette, Annunziata, and Anna, my much older brothers Julius and Ed, my slightly older brother John, and my younger brothers Paul and Al. Quite a brood.

The Brancas at the Polo Grounds that spring afternoon included Rosemary, Margaret, and Suzanne, who, like Mom, not only enjoyed the lowered admission that came with Ladies' Day—I believe it was 50 cents—but also loved baseball as much as we boys. Mom kept an immaculate box score. The fact that she had been born in Sandorf, a village sixty miles from Budapest, and arrived on these shores in 1900 had not prevented her from assimilating into American culture with amazing grace. (Only recently have I learned that my mother was actually born Jewish and converted to Catholicism. She never mentioned this to us, but it may explain my extraordinarily deep love of Jewish people.)

Mom spoke English with only a wisp of an accent. Among many talents, she had learned to cook Italian with a flare that had my father's side of the family raving. She also kept her Hungarian cooking talents intact. She was worldly wise, down to earth, loving, and practical. She handled our meager money with remarkable resourcefulness. She'd get a free meat bone that the butcher was ready to discard and work it into a fabulous tomato-based soup that, with a couple of loaves of Italian bread and a lettuce salad, would feed us for two days. If anyone possessed domestic genius, it was my mother. She had met Dad—a man of all trades and master of many—when she took the trolley in Harlem. He was the conductor. She was 15, he was 20. Every time I hear the story of their meeting, I think of Judy Garland singing "The Trolley Song" in the MGM musical *Meet Me in St. Louis*.

My relationship with sports was rooted in family, warmth, and love, but it also had something to do with math. I was a statistics fanatic. At an early age, I understood the mathematical basis of a pitcher's earned-run average. I could reel off the rosters of all the teams in major league baseball, football, and basketball. I played all those sports—and so did my brothers. At times our little house up in Mount Vernon looked like Grand Central Station, bustling with kids of all ages hustling to get to their games on time.

After the last game of the Giant/Cardinal doubleheader was over, my family and I headed for the exits. Before we left the ballpark, I turned around to take in the vastness of the field one more time. Empty of its players, it seemed peaceful and perfectly beautiful. I dreamed the dream—that eternal American Dream dreamed by millions—that one day I'd be on that field. I'd get to run on that grass. I'd get to take that mound.

What I did not know, though—what no one short of God Almighty could have known—was that this strangely shaped ballpark, with all its illogical widths and dark depths, would, in only 15 short years, be the very scene that, at least in the minds of many, would define my life. How I spent these next 15 years, how I arrived at that moment, is the tale I will tell now.

League of Nations

M Y PARENTS MOVED from Harlem to Mount Vernon to raise a family. Dad wanted a little house and yard for gardening. He left his post as a conductor and became a barber in a tiny two-man shop on Sandford Boulevard and Sixth Avenue, three blocks from where we lived on Ninth. He loved fixing cars. He loved working as an electrician, plumber, house painter—you name it and Dad did it. He loved sawing the logs that the Department of Public Works dropped off for us to heat our potbellied stove in the kitchen and the furnace in the cellar. At various times all his sons struggled to outsaw him, but we couldn't come close. Dad would not be defeated. He would not stop working. Even during the Depression, when money was scarce and feeding his huge family a Herculean task, he refused home relief. No welfare for Dad. He was Mr. Self-Reliance, a quiet man who had been born in the town of Lappano in the province of Cosenza in Calabria, a region in the boot of Italy. When Dad married Mom, his dad—Raffaelo—became a permanent part of the family and lived with us until he passed in 1945 at age 95.

Raffaelo had originally come to the United States with his twin, Frank, in 1873, when they worked for the Northern Pacific Railroad in Minnesota and the Dakotas. Grandpa told stories of freezing-cold winter mornings when they were putting down steel

9

tracks. The work was rough and the bosses demanding. But the real challenge came, he said, when they heard the fierce war cries of Indians descending from the hills. In the days before television, to hear an account—especially from your own flesh and blood—of bows-and-arrows battles was all the entertainment we required. Grandpa also liked to dramatize his postrailroad days when he moved to East Harlem, and from there to Argentina, only to return to Italy, where he married Anna Sanserverino. Their son John, my father, was born in 1880. My dad had a brother Frank, a sister Maggie, who died when I was an infant, and a second sister, Rose, who became an important part of my life. Aunt Rose was among the first teachers of Italian descent in the New York public schools, where she taught from 1910 to 1970.

The first remarkable fact about my unremarkable childhood in Mount Vernon is that, with one exception, I cannot remember an incident of racial prejudice.

The second remarkable fact about this same unremarkable childhood is that I cannot—without a single exception—recall a major incident of family dysfunction.

I cannot explain the absence of what has become standard fare for a first-generation autobiographical narrative rooted in the thirties and forties of the previous century. I wouldn't at all mind spicing up this story with some sensational episodes—if only I had any. The simple truth is that in Mount Vernon, this plain city no bigger than four square miles and some 60,000 citizens, I was taught to love my neighbors and, because I knew no better, I did just that.

Our neighbor was Ben Lichtenfeld, a Jew who owned a junkyard directly across the street. He paid us by the pound to collect papers and metals. A couple of times I placed a rock or two inside the paper pile, but no one's perfect. I think Ben knew the neighborhood kids did that, but he deliberately ignored it. Grandma Lichtenfeld paid us to light her stove on the Sabbath. In my home, I didn't hear a bad word spoken about Jews. Far as I was concerned, Jews were *paisans,* to be respected as we were taught to respect the

Amarusos, the Ligouris, the Tartaglias, and the Cerones, and the O'Farrells and the Formans.

Our next-door neighbors were the Smiths, and up the block lived the Tuckers, Levinsons, and Woodsons—all African Americans. We walked the streets together; we played ball together; we were welcome in their homes and they were welcome in ours.

I understand that although we were only a quarter mile from the Bronx, we were spared the discomfort of overcrowded immigrant life in New York City. Although a working-class city, Mount Vernon was largely a collection of small neighborhoods of single houses. In contrast, tenement living breeds traumas and toxins, emotional and otherwise. We were blessed to have escaped the tenements. Space—even when you're poor—is a luxury. Space also is relative, because in our house the kids had to sleep two or three to a bed.

The single incident of prejudice came when I was 14. I wanted to go to high school for a full three years, not the usual two. The kids from the south side of Mount Vernon—our side, the poor side—went for only two because our school, A. B. Davis, didn't consider us college material. That meant we were denied an additional year of sports, thus reducing our chances for scholarships. As a teenager, though, I already had other ideas. My Aunt Rose, a teacher and crusader for women's rights, who lived near Gramercy Park in Manhattan but came to visit us often, always stressed education. I'd been told I had a 160 IQ, and many adults, especially my older brother Julie, had instilled in me the idea that I could achieve on the highest level. I was intrigued by math, science, and mechanics. I was planning on becoming an engineer—that is, until I entered the office of Miss Lorraine Birch.

She was a severe woman of few words. When I explained my goals, she got right to the point.

"Nonsense," she said. "I know your family, and you won't be going to college. You aren't college material, and they can't afford it."

In those days kids didn't argue with teachers. At the same time,

I'm a natural-born contrarian. When I'm pushed, I push back. I had to say something.

"Why aren't I college material?" I asked.

"It's not in your background."

"I'm in the A group of my class," I reminded her.

"It's good to be in the A group of your eighth-grade class," she said. "But that has no bearing on college. College requires intellectual vigor. You'll do well to avoid math, science, and a foreign language and stick with the basics. Take shop. You people are good with your hands."

Part of me wishes I had choked her with my hands. But I was a kid, only 14, and ultimately did what she said. I didn't take science or math. I chose not to study a language. I dropped my plans to become an engineer. She didn't quash my desire to go to college completely—later, under amazing circumstances, I *would* attend—but at this critical juncture the woman stomped on a dream.

Sometimes I wonder why I didn't fight back. My parents' understanding of the American school system was limited, so I know why I didn't go to them. How about Aunt Rose? I thought that she'd side with her colleague the teacher. I figured that just as jocks stuck together, teachers did, too. But I was probably wrong; Aunt Rose would have encouraged me to take the courses. I wish I could have gone to Julie, my oldest brother. Along with John, Julie was my biggest booster. Julie would have given that witch a piece of his mind. But Julie had gone off to fight for his country. He had more important things to do than worry about my problems with a school counselor. I succumbed. I followed the noncollege prep program set out for me. It's one of the few moments of my life when, in the face of blind prejudice, I caved.

Did Miss Birch discourage me because my name ends in a vowel? I sure as hell think so. Why else? My grades were great, my motivation keen, and my goal reasonable. In her mind, though, certain ethnic groups had their place. Italian Americans were manual laborers, not college students. And that was that.

In addition to the absence of racial animus in our household, there was no animus among the Brancas. Maybe it was the remarkable character of our parents—a devoted mother who kept the books, a devoted father who worked nonstop. Or maybe it was the peculiar sibling structure. For the boys—for John, me, Paul, and Al—we had three dads. Our real dad, plus brothers Julie and Ed, who were wonderful surrogate fathers. They were, in fact, old enough to be our fathers and certainly gave us the attention that Dad, busy at work, couldn't. They not only taught us ball, they also taught us life. They were tough guys, but never violent. Their toughness was manifest in manly competition, but not in the street. This was the pregang era of American life when your primary identification was with family. You protected family at all costs.

I was only four or five when I watched Julie play ball. He played with enormous authority and strength. I remember the time he fell and broke his nose. When they rushed him to the hospital, I got to go along. As the doctor was resetting the bone, I sat on the bed next to him, my hand on the sleeve of his uniform. Nearly 80 years later, I can still feel the warmth of that woolen jersey. The jersey represented the world to me, pride in my brother, and the possibility of one day being like him. In my mind, he had mastered this magnificent game of baseball. And as I inched closer to him, I could hear his silent message being sent my way: *play hard, give it all you got, and if you get hurt, suck it up.* For all the pain he felt in his face that day, he never uttered a sound.

The role model of my era was *Jack Armstrong, the All-American Boy*, a radio show sponsored by Wheaties, Breakfast of Champions. Jack set the tone: You don't drink or cheat, you walk the straight and narrow, you display courage and cunning and, if need be, you save the damsel in distress. I wanted to be Jack. At times I thought I was.

Twelve siblings—plus a mother, father, and grandfather—are a lot to cram into one house, but we did it. Necessity is the mother of invention, and my mother was wonderfully creative in creating a loving home. Naturally, there were hurt feelings from time to time, but not deep wounds. Later, when I became the first in the family to gain a degree of fame, you might have expected at least a little sibling rivalry. But it never happened. The Brancas stuck together. We took on the world as one.

This sense of psychological stability surely had something to do with the divine spirit guiding us. We were raised believing Catholics. Our church, St. Francis of Assisi, was just a block away, named for a man who said, "For it is in giving that we receive." Christ entered my heart, and has remained there, with the simple clarity of His message: be kind, be compassionate. As a little boy I learned that He had given up his life to help others. I embraced His story and holy mission. I accepted His love. I still attend Mass every Sunday.

Everyone in the Branca household worked. As a school kid, I worked at Kaplan's Kosher Meat Market washing produce that had been handpicked by Mr. D'Agostino, the same gentleman who would make his name with a chain of high-end grocery stores across the region. Later I'd hitchhike the Bronx River Parkway to Tuckahoe, where I got a dollar a bag, and a quarter tip, to be a caddy. That was my first exposure to seeing how the other side lived.

Like my sisters and brothers, I always contributed to the household and, with my leftover change, might go to the movies to see *Tarzan* or run over to Woolworth's to buy live baby chicks, three for a dime.

Other than ball games, there were no excursions to Manhattan except for the occasional trip with Mom to S. Klein, a huge bulk of a discount store that dominated busy Union Square. A couple of times a year each sibling would get a few items of new clothing.

FDR took office in 1933, when I was seven. My folks sang his

praises. I grew up in a household of FDR Democrats. That influence would have a far greater impact on my brother John, who
would one day become a state legislator, not to mention chairman
of the New York State Athletic Commission. I recall our family
sitting by the radio and listening to Roosevelt's Fireside Chats.

Compared to the other shows, though—*Jack Benny, Burns and
Allen, Dick Tracy, Fibber McGee and Molly, The Shadow*, and *Amos
'n' Andy*—the president was boring. Like everything else in my
young life, radio was most exciting when it focused on sports.

My brothers and I, for instance, were huddled around the radio
in December 1934 when, once again, the Polo Grounds loomed
large in my imagination. On this frosty afternoon when ice covered the field, the football Giants were facing the Chicago Bears
and their star running back, Bronco Nagurski, in only the second
annual NFL championship game. Back in those pre–Super Bowl
days, this was as super as any game got.

At halftime, with all the slipping and sliding, the Giants were
losing 10–3 when someone suggested they trade their cleats for
sneakers. An equipment man scrambled over to Manhattan College to find some. The Giants wound up wearing basketball shoes
and, led by quarterback Ed Danowski, already a local hero for his
athletic feats at Fordham, won 30–13. I'm sure being there was an
experience no one will ever forget, but I cherish those hours spent
with my ear to the radio, my mind filled with pictures painted by
announcers. They were our poets, just as surely as in years to come
Red Barber and Vince Scully would become poets of the Dodgers.
We hung on their every burst of enthusiasm and cry of frustration.
I went to sleep that night dreaming of the Polo Grounds, a green
lawn in summer, a frozen tundra in winter.

As a family, the Brancas were essentially homebodies. Our
orbit was small: work, school, sports, church. Our notion of a good
time on a Saturday night was singing songs around the fireplace.
We had a player piano and, in brother Eddie, someone who played
by ear. We'd harmonize on the great World War I anthem "Over

There" and the cornball ballads of the day—"John Took Me Home to See His Mother" and "The White Cliffs of Dover." We all could sing, but I like to think that my own voice, even at a young age, had bottom and range. And, man, did I love to belt it out! At Christmastime I was a committed caroler. Later in life I'd take my singing seriously and even toy with a career in show business.

From the thirties through the forties, the big bands—Benny Goodman, Artie Shaw, Glenn Miller, the Dorsey Brothers—had us dancing through a time of political uncertainty with a steady swing. Helen O'Connell, Bing Crosby, and Frank Sinatra crooned with a sweetness that took the edge off the daily life of a country on the brink of another world war.

That war, of course, changed everything and became the defining event of our generation. It was a war of unprecedented loss and tragedy, but also a war of great clarity. The line between good and bad was writ large. It was the last unambiguous American war. The moral and political issues were plain. Evil had run amok, and evil had to be crushed. It was a noble fight to the death, a cause, an absolute imperative.

Every American household felt the impact of what was happening in Europe and Asia. The Branca household was no exception. The Brancas, along with the rest of the country, made the shift. At the end of the thirties, we were in war mode.

Teenage Tryouts

FORGET WHATEVER MODERN connotations the word "teenager" brings to mind. In the thirties and forties, the age group from 13 to 19 wasn't seen as a distinct category. That would come in the fifties—when teens challenged the age of conformity—and the sixties—when teen rebellion found its fullest expression. The forties was the war decade. Teens signed up, went to battle, and risked their lives. Millions of teen boys like myself coveted adulthood and adult responsibilities. We wanted to grow up. We yearned to serve. The culture of impassioned patriotism informed our every move. We wanted to prove ourselves on the field of combat. And if we were either too young or disqualified from the armed services, we'd take that energy—that sense of do or die—to the field of sports.

I was a tall, skinny kid with strong legs and a big butt. At about age 11, I shot up from 5'6" to 5'11". My growth spurt went on for a few years until I reached 6'3". Among my brothers, I was the only one to grow so tall. And if you wanted to be a pitcher—and, believe me, we all did—height helped. Physically, I lucked out.

My training had been intense. Before Julie had gone off to the army, he'd raised us on the sandlots and in our driveway. We'd been in the midget and junior leagues. In the thirties, my older brother Eddie named our team the Vanderbilts—Vandies for short.

He thought that the name connoted class, and at some point all the Branca boys were active Vandies. As teens, John and I pitched for A. B. Davis, the same high school where our younger brothers Paul and Al would both follow us to the mound. John, Paul, and Al wound up throwing in Class B ball. Pitching was in our blood. We were bonded in an unbreakable brotherhood, devoted to victory overseas and victory on the ball field. Loss was unacceptable. As competitors, we were fierce.

Brother John and I had our ears glued to the radio. It was a Sunday afternoon in early December 1941, and our football Giants were getting pounded by the Brooklyn Dodgers, an NFL team that played from 1930 to 1943 in Ebbets Field, a faraway ballpark I'd never seen. So far as I was concerned, Brooklyn was on the other side of the moon. The Polo Grounds, though, was on *our* side of the moon, and the Polo Grounds was the scene of this game. I could see it all in my head, the horseshoe-shaped ballpark, the packed stands, the hard dirt of the playing field turned brown by winter's freeze.

At one point, John and I could hear the public address announcer begin to make a series of requests:

"Lieutenant Joe Smith—report to the information office immediately."

"Sergeant Clarence Jones—come to the information office immediately."

"Calling Colonel Richard Pace to the information office."

The announcements kept coming. The commentators broadcasting the game didn't say anything, but John and I knew something was wrong.

The next day, our family was huddled around that same radio as we heard President Roosevelt say, "Yesterday, December 7, 1941—a date which will live in infamy—the United States of America was suddenly and deliberately attacked by naval and air forces of the Empire of Japan." The words that stirred us most were: "No matter how long it may take us to overcome this pre-meditated invasion, the American people in their righteous might will win through to absolute victory, so help us God!"

Pearl Harbor set the wheels in motion. By the summer of '42, with the world at war, Julius had joined the army and Eddie was in the air corps. My big brothers, in their thirties, had rushed to enlist. The next year, when I turned 17, I planned to join the navy V-12 program. I wanted to fight.

Something else happened in the summer of 1942, though, that took me by surprise. Our sister Anna, having followed our careers at A. B. Davis, where John and I were star pitchers, took the initiative to write the three major league teams in our area—the Giants, Yankees, and Dodgers—to ask about their recruitment plans and policies. A week later, she heard back. All three organizations invited us to their tryouts.

For us, the first was the best. We were set to pitch on those hallowed grounds—the Polo Grounds—object of my earliest fantasies. In the pre-TV world of baseball, there was far less hype surrounding major leaguers. Sure, the stars were larger than life, but the workaday players were regular guys with regular salaries. If you had some talent, some fortitude, and a will to win, those jobs appeared to be attainable. During the war years, the game felt especially local and accessible. Without excessive arrogance or conceit, I could see the trajectory of my career—going from the midget leagues to the junior leagues to the Vandies to a high school championship and then on to the great New York Giants. In my mind, such an accomplishment wasn't far-fetched.

John and I shared a bed, and I can't remember who got up first that morning, but it wasn't much past the crack of dawn. This was the day of days. We dressed in a hurry, wolfed down cold cereal, and grabbed our baseball equipment. I had more heat than John, but John had more finesse. In a future era when Greg Maddux became the first pitcher to win 15 games in 17 straight seasons by using unerring control as opposed to overwhelming power, John might have found his mark. What John lacked in speed, he made up in movement. I loved to catch him and watch his pitches jump. He loved to catch me, never failing to encourage my every pitch.

Now, I know that sibling rivalry is a staple in Psychology 101. I know that in a family of this many children you'd presume we were all vying for attention. You'd think there wasn't enough of our parents' time or love to go around. You'd think that at some point we kids would be looking for ways to undercut each other.

Wrong.

Sure, I wanted to be chosen, but I wanted my brother to be chosen just as badly. And he felt the same. He told me so, and I know by his actions that he meant it. When he was the quarterback on our high school football team, I was an end. I caught his passes. I could read his eyes and see where he wanted to throw. He could read my feet and see where I wanted to run. We were inseparable. Together, we were unbeatable.

As we headed toward the bus that would take us to the subway, we felt moisture in the air. Looked like rain. We wished the rain away, but the rain didn't cooperate. By the time we reached the Polo Grounds, it was coming down cats and dogs. Tryouts postponed. Come back tomorrow.

Tomorrow couldn't come soon enough. Another restless night, another crack-of-dawn awakening. Another walk to the bus, a bus ride to the subway, the subway to the Polo Grounds—only this time the sky had cleared and sunlight poured from the heavens. Sunlight was blessing this day when brother John and I were going to pitch in the Polo Grounds and prove to our beloved New York Giants that we had what it took.

Just to step out onto the field itself was a tremendous charge. After all, this was the field I had viewed so many times from the upper deck and distant bleachers. This was the field where I'd watched Mel Ott—now the team's player/manager—terrify opposing pitchers, the field where the football Giants had pum-

meled the Bears. This was the field of my dreams—and the
dreams of at least 300 other boys who were there to try out. We
were amazed that out of those 300 at least 70 were pitchers. The
competition was keen. The Giants' coach was Adolfo Domingo
de Guzman "Dolf" Luque, one of the first Cubans to play major
league ball. He'd been a starting pitcher for the Boston Braves,
the Reds, the Dodgers, and the Giants. Luque knew his stuff. He
was a light-skinned, blue-eyed Latino fireball who made it clear
what he was looking for—heat, heat, and more heat. "Throw
hard as you can," he said. "Pour it on. We want to see your top
speed. If you don't show us what you got today, there ain't no
tomorrow."

Luque asked the pitchers to line up. John and I were at the
end of the line. I watched carefully. I knew I threw close to 90,
and I also knew that most of the young men throwing couldn't
match my speed. I was eager to prove myself. Each candidate got
to throw some 20 pitches. That's all I needed. I tried to be patient,
but it was hard. Some of the guys took a long time to settle in and
start their routine. Some had no business being there. Others were
impressive. John came before me, and when he was finally given
the nod to run out to the mound, I was relieved. I was rooting for
him all the way. He placed his pitches well. He threw with control. His speed, while not great, was more than adequate. He did
himself proud. When he trotted back and stood next to me, I pat-
ted him on the back and said, "Great job." He smiled and replied,
"You're going to do even better."

Except I didn't. I didn't do anything at all. After John, the
tryouts ended. We weren't told why, when, or if they'd be resumed
on another day. We were simply told to go.

"If we need to get in touch with any of you kids," said Luque,
"we have your numbers."

"Wait a minute," John protested, "my brother Ralph didn't get
a chance to throw. He throws harder than anyone who's been out
there today."

21

"Sorry for your brother," said Luque, "but he'll have to come back another time. This tryout session is over."

John started to say something else, but the coach had turned his back and was walking off the field.

"No big deal," I said to John.

"What are you talking about, Ralph? It's a helluva big deal. You never pitched. They don't know what they're missing."

"Don't worry, I'll get to pitch. Anna set up tryouts with the Yankees and Dodgers."

"But what about the Giants?"

"You got the chance to pitch for the Giants, John. At least one Branca got out there. I'm sure they'll call you back."

John didn't hear back from the Giants, but that didn't discourage us.

A week later we were at Yankee Stadium. The Stadium didn't have the familiarity of the Polo Grounds. It felt a bit like foreign territory. It was primarily where we went to watch Joe D play. Only the year before—1941—Joe D had hit .357. That sounds terrific, until you remember that during the same year Ted Williams hit .406—and Bob Feller won 25 games and struck out 260. These numbers were rattling around my head—my brain was always stuffed with stats—when I was finally tapped, for the first time ever, to pitch in front of a major league coach. His name was Charles Albert Bender, and among baseball aficionados like myself, he was famous. He was a future Hall of Fame pitcher, a half-Chippewa Indian who had broken in with the Philadelphia Athletics at the start of the century. At 6'2", he was an imposing man who went by the name Chief Bender. Ty Cobb had called him one of the best pitchers ever.

"What's your best pitch, kid?" Chief Bender asked me as I took the mound.

"Fastball," I said.

"You have any other pitches?" he wanted to know.

"A curve—and also an overhand curve that I call a drop."

"Let's see your drop."

Chief Bender saw it once, then asked to see it again. In all, I threw three near-perfect drops.

"You said you had a fastball," he said. "Show me."

I reared back and fired five straight burners. There were no speed clocks, but I'm guessing high 80s. Chief Bender looked impressed.

"How old are you?" he asked.

"Sixteen," I said.

"Sixteen's too young," Chief Bender told me. "But 17 isn't. Come back next year when you're 17."

"And you won't forget me?"

"Indians don't forget anything. Branca. *Ralph Branca.* You'll hear from me."

I never did.

The third and last tryout Anna had set up was with the Dodgers. I considered the Dodgers a long shot because I felt no emotional connection with them. The Giants and Yankees played in our backyard. The Dodgers played on Mars. Truth is, when John and I went to Sheepshead Bay, the bay that separates mainland Brooklyn from eastern Coney Island, I was entering the borough for the first time. It was a long trip—at 26.2 miles the longest subway ride you can take, all for a nickel. (As of this writing, the fare is $2.50.) The cars, by the way, had seats made of real cane and, if it was crowded, you held on to handles of real wood. We stayed on the Lexington Avenue line to Grand Central, shuttled over to Times Square, and then rode the BMT deep into Brooklyn, where we got off at Surf Avenue.

We walked over to a ballpark called Celtic Oval that, oddly enough, had its right-field fence on rollers. During games they pushed back the fence across the street to extend the range for a home run. This was where the Dodgers were having tryouts. Two scouting coaches—Joe Labate and Jimmy Ferrante—looked us over. There weren't nearly as many kids as there'd been in the Polo Grounds or Yankee Stadium. John and I each got to throw about 40 pitches. When we were through, Labate came over to me and said, "Ever been to Ebbets Field?"

"No, sir."

"So you're not a Brooklyn boy."

"Mount Vernon," I said.

"But you'll be able to find your way to Ebbets Field if you have to."

"Yes, sir."

"Well, show up next Tuesday. Get there early. You're pitching batting practice."

"I am?"

"What's the matter? Don't you think you can handle it?" he asked.

"I know I can."

The ride home seemed to take a lot less time than the ride going. John was so excited for me. Even though he hadn't been selected to throw batting practice, we agreed that one day he would. John was a helluva pitcher. He knew how to set up hitters and had the control to finish them off. When we got home, John did most of the talking, bragging about me. Our family was so ecstatic that you would have thought I'd been signed.

Sometime in August 1942, before a regularly scheduled Dodger game, I walked into Ebbets Field for the first time. I would later remember my dear friend Vince Scully, the longtime broadcaster of the Dodgers, saying this about Ebbets Field: "At other ballparks the crowd is like wallpaper. All the faces merge together into an anonymous landscape. Ebbets was radically different. Because the facility itself was so small, the minute you stepped inside you felt an intimacy. You didn't see a crowd, you saw individuals. The distance between the playing field and the stands was negligible. The fans were practically on the field. The players smelled the breath of the fans, and the fans smelled the breath of the players. The dialogue between those who came to cheer—or boo—and those who came to play was incredibly familiar. Every game at Ebbets Field was like old home week, a neighborhood meeting, a get-together among friends who knew and loved each other well enough to say whatever they wanted."

The facts were these: the Polo Grounds had room for 56,000 fans; Yankee Stadium, 67,000; and Ebbets Field, 32,000 (with room for another 3,000 or 4,000 fanatics who didn't mind standing in the aisles or on the rooftops of neighboring apartment buildings). Plunked down smack in the center of the working-class neighborhood of Flatbush, Ebbets Field had opened in 1913, when the team roster included outfielder Casey Stengel, who made the catch of the day. The Dodgers lost anyway to the Phils, 1–0.

Walking through Flatbush, you came upon Ebbets Field like you'd come upon a local candy store, a Jewish deli, or an Italian grocery. Ebbets Field was in and of itself a local character—unassuming and unpretentious. Yankee Stadium was and is monumental. The Polo Grounds was bizarrely sculpted, with an endless center field and imposing overhanging stands. Ebbets Field wasn't bizarre. It was comforting and ordinary. It was a happy resident in a residential neighborhood. Most everyone walked there or took the train. If you drove, you were lucky to find a spot in the one small parking lot, on Montgomery Street. Players paid attendants at nearby gas stations to watch their cars.

Built at the intersection of Bedford Avenue (in back of the crazy 38-foot-high wall and in-play screen of right field), Montgomery Street (behind left field), Sullivan Place (that backed up on home plate), and McKeever Place (beyond third base), Ebbets Field wasn't a basilica or a cathedral; it wasn't a great mosque or an imposing synagogue; it was a down-the-street storefront church where anyone could come in and feel the love.

I'm not sure I was feeling the love when I stepped onto the playing field in August 1942 to pitch batting practice. I was feeling fear. Even though my job was simply to get the ball over the plate so the hitters could loosen up and tune their timing, I was a little flustered. It wasn't that anyone was paying attention to me. The fans were just filtering in. Many of the superstars were off serving our country, but the hitters I faced were names I knew. As I pitched to catcher Mickey Owen, I couldn't help but remember what had happened in last year's World Series, right here in Ebbets Field, between the Dodgers and Yankees. The moment was already part of New York baseball lore:

October 5, 1941. Yanks were up two games to one. Dodgers leading in the top of the ninth, 4–3. Bases empty, two out. Three more strikes and Brooklyn would tie the Series. Big Hugh Casey on the mound. Tommy Henrich at the plate. Henrich swung at an overhead curve and missed by a mile. Game was over. . . . But wait . . .

. . . the unexpected pitch got away from Mickey Owen. It was a passed ball, and Henrich was safe at first. Then the Bombers fired away: Joe D singled, Charlie Keller doubled, and the Yanks were ahead 5–4. By the time the inning was over, they were winning 7–4. The Dodgers went down 1-2-3 in the ninth, New York won the game, and the next day closed out the Series, four to one.

For a while, Mickey was a goat in Brooklyn. Insiders, though, knew it wasn't Mickey's fault. No catcher could have handled that big breaking slider, which even might have been a spitter. I knew that the Dodger fans were forgiving, because the same afternoon I pitched batting practice Owen was introduced over the PA system to rousing cheers. As the years have gone by, though, I've noticed that any time Mickey's name is mentioned, I hear the same comment: "Oh, that guy who missed the ball that cost Brooklyn the Series."

Strange how a single play can define an entire career. I remember thinking that day on the mound in Ebbets Field, *Man, I'd hate for anything like that to ever happen to me.*

In '42, in spite of that bitter defeat in October '41, Dodger fans were hopeful. Their Bums were in a pennant race with the Stan Musial/Enos Slaughter Cardinals. The Dodgers would lose by only two games, but the team, revitalized when the pugnacious Leo Durocher took over as manager, had become a perennial contender. "Wait till next year!" became the Brooklyn battle cry. With a single exception, that cry was applicable for 15 years—the remainder of the club's tenure in the borough described by poet Walt Whitman as the "city of homes and churches."

My debut as a batting practice pitcher in the summer of 1942 was of note to no one except my brother, my family, my friends, and myself. I'd done my job; I put the ball over the plate. The hitters hit at will. They pulverized my pitches. I received neither criticism nor praise from the Dodger organization that, like the Yankees, said that they would be in touch. So it was back to school.

I was a junior that year, John a senior, and we were both pitching aces for the A. B. Davis baseball squad. John made the *New York Journal-American* All-Star team and didn't lose a game all season. He was 12–0 and I was 2–0. When it came time for the Mount Vernon Senior League Baseball championship—a best of five—we were tied 2–2. Because I had pitched batting practice for the Dodgers, I thought I should get the nod to pitch the rubber match. My head was still a little swollen from that afternoon in Ebbets Field. John got the nod instead and unfortunately lost 1–0. He was still my hero. He joined the air corps and, before long, served in Japan. I longed to do the same.

I also longed to play professional ball, which is why I decided to double up my high school courses, graduate early, enlist in the navy through their V-12 program, fulfill my patriotic obligation as a pilot, get out, and pitch. I did graduate in June 1943, and I did well on all the navy tests. Nonetheless, they rejected me because of asthma and a punctured eardrum. No worries. When I turned 18 in January, the army was sure to draft me.

Then came good news: the Dodgers had me back to Ebbets Field, where I pitched batting practice again, this time before an exhibition game with the Yankees.

As spring turned to summer, a letter came to our home at 522 South Ninth Avenue, Mount Vernon, New York. The return address read, "Brooklyn Dodgers, 215 Montague Street, Brooklyn, New York." The message was clear: *Come to the office. Branch Rickey, the general manager, wants to see you. P.S. Because you are underage, please bring an adult who is authorized to sign for you. Time is of the essence.*

A week later my mother and I were in downtown Brooklyn, walking past Borough Hall, on our way to the Dodger front office. We were shown to a waiting room with leather couches and over-stuffed armchairs. The walls were covered with photos of famous Dodgers, from Casey Stengel to Pete Reiser. I knew them all. I knew their stats. But I knew absolutely nothing about the behind-the-scenes executives and owners. All I knew is that I wanted to play ball.

After waiting 20 minutes, Mom and I were escorted into the wood-paneled office of the general manager and president of the Brooklyn Dodgers. Branch Rickey commanded the room. He sat in a high-back judge's chair in back of a huge mahogany desk. He had big bushy eyebrows and bright eyes that scrutinized us with a single glance. He did not smile. He sucked on an unlit cigar and leaned back in his chair. The black bow tie around his neck bobbled as he said the words, "Good afternoon. I trust this will be the start of a mutually beneficial relationship."

At the time of our meeting, here's what I didn't know: that Branch Rickey had once been an unsuccessful major league catcher; that he had run the St. Louis Cardinals during the "Gashouse Gang" days of Dizzy and Daffy Dean; that he had initiated the first comprehensive farm club system in baseball; that he was a deeply devout Methodist; that the press called him the Mahatma and the Deacon; that he had been compared to a U.S. Supreme Court justice; that he held degrees in art, literature, and law; that he had an enormous ego; that his devotion to the sport he loved was matched only by his devotion to making money; that although he refused to attend games on Sunday, the Lord's day, he never failed to check on the attendance; that his deal with the Dodgers gave him 10 percent of team profits, thus motivating him to be as penurious with players as possible; that, of all the owners with reputations for being skinflints—the Comiskeys in Chicago, the Griffiths in Washington, Sam Breadon in St. Louis, Sid Weill in Cincy—Rickey was the stingiest.

"Mrs. Branca," he said, "we'd like your son Ralph to play for our farm team in Olean. The pay is $90 a month. What do you say?"

"Say 'yes,' Mom," I said.

Rickey broke out into a smile. "You have an eager boy there, Mrs. Branca."

"Yes," she said. "He wants to play baseball."

"Then we are in agreement?" he asked.

"We are," Mom answered, quickly signing the document set before her.

In essence, the document bound me to the Dodgers for life. The infamous reserve clause meant I was theirs until they chose to release or trade me. Of course, I could always ask to be released or traded, but the decision to say yea or nay belonged to them, not me. The legal restriction's one-sided bias led to ridiculous scenarios—like the time when Dizzy Dean, having retired from the Cubs, was broadcasting for the Cards and wanted to play in an old-timers' game in a Cards uniform, but couldn't until the Cubs gave him a release. Talk about being handcuffed! Until Curt Flood's brave challenge galvanized his fellow athletes, this clause enslaved players in baseball and all other major professional sports.

Slave or not, I was ready to go. In 1944, the Dodgers fielded some 875 minor leaguers on 35 different teams. I was sent to one of the lesser ones, the Olean Oilers of the Class D Pennsylvania-Ontario-New York (P.O.N.Y.) League. It was a job, my first as a pro. I would have gone anywhere.

Forget glamour. Forget comfort. Forget adventure. I was told to show up at Grand Central, where a slow-moving overnight train took me and teammate Billy DeMars, another teenager, a fine shortstop and future big league coach, to far western New York. We shared an upper berth and, given the tight quarters, kept falling out of bed. It was an inauspicious beginning to an inauspicious summer.

Olean was a small town off the Allegheny River in Cattaraugus County, population 12,000. The games were uneventful and I did not distinguish myself. The ballpark itself was probably in worse shape than my high school playing field. We rode a broken-down bus to the out-of-town games in Bradford, Jamestown; Lockport, Batavia; and Wellsville. Mercifully, the minor leagues shut down after Labor Day, and I was back in my parents' home.

Despite the admonitions of counselor Lorraine Birch, I had decided to go to college. I was accepted at New York University where I enrolled in September 1943, and played both basketball and baseball for the NYU Violets. I was determined to get an education—and also to keep honing my skills as a jock.

I was one determined kid.

I was also one heartbroken kid when, after my 18th birthday in January 1944, I saw my one chance to serve the country collapse. Like the navy, the army turned me down, giving the same reasons—asthma and punctured eardrum. At a time when the radio was playing Kay Kyser's "Praise the Lord and the Pass the

Ammunition" and the Song Spinners' "Comin' in on a Wing and a Prayer," I was crashing. Emotionally, I was spent. My brothers were doing their part. Julie was in the army, Eddie and John in the army air corps; soon Paul would join the air corps, and Al would serve in the army, where for many years he worked as a science instructor. I felt like an outcast.

I persevered. Took the bus and subway every weekday from Mount Vernon down to the Greenwich Village campus of NYU. I made excellent grades and excelled at sports. I was called teacher's pet because when the college baseball team drove to out-of-town games, coach Bill McCarthy let me ride in his car. He thought I had promise as a player and even mentioned me to his brother, Dr. Ralph McCarthy, team physician for the Boston Red Sox.

"Ralph was at one of our games and saw you pitch," Bill told me. "He feels sure he can get you a $10,000 signing bonus with Boston."

My jaw dropped. Saying $10,000 in 1944 was like saying half a million today. Of course, what Coach McCarthy didn't know was that I was already signed to the Dodgers. Had I told him that, I wouldn't be able to play for NYU.

"I gotta confess something, coach," I heard myself saying.

"You sound like George Washington about to confess to cutting down the cherry tree," said McCarthy.

I told him the truth, that I had been paid to play in Olean. McCarthy understood. He wasn't angry, but explained that I could no longer play for NYU. He was still willing, though, to put me in touch with his brother. He suggested that I ask someone in my family to go with me and ask Rickey for my release.

That was early May. In June, when my brother Julius came home on leave, I asked him to accompany me to Rickey's office. Julie, who'd do anything for his little brothers, readily agreed. Julie was an impressive guy—and a serviceman to boot.

•

31

The door to Rickey's office was shut tight as we waited in the outer chamber a long time. Julius looked sharp in his freshly ironed uniform and smart army cap. From the other side of the door we heard muffled voices. Finally, when the door opened, eight or ten reporters came filing out. I heard several of them comment:

"Rickey's a genius, isn't he?"

"He's always good copy. Always has something clever to say."

"You can never get in the last word with that guy."

A few minutes later, Rickey, with his unlit cigar and bulging bow tie, was leaning back in his judge's chair. He seemed glad to see us.

"Good morning, gentlemen," he said. "This is a fine morning to sign a new contract."

My brother asked the nature of the contract.

Rickey said it was for one year—to play for the Brooklyn Dodgers, at $400 a month.

"With a bonus?" asked Julius.

"A bonus?" Rickey repeated. "Oh, I'm afraid not. Your brother, as promising as he is, has not demonstrated enough to justify a bonus. Bonuses are rare commodities these days."

"Well, sir," said Julie, "we feel sure that the Boston Red Sox are prepared to offer Ralph a $10,000 bonus. We'd like to ask that you release him so that he might get that bonus."

"Release him? That'd be foolish of me. Your brother's a jewel—a jewel-in-the-rough, to be sure—but a jewel nonetheless."

"If you don't release him, could you match Boston's bonus?" asked Julie.

"And turn myself into an even greater fool? I hardly think so. Why should I pay an exorbitant bonus when contractually your brother is obligated to this organization without a bonus? That would be extraordinarily bad business. And when it comes to business, sir, I pride myself on being sharp, not dull. You're asking me to negotiate against myself."

"I'm asking you to think of Ralph," said Julie.

"I am thinking of Ralph. And what I think is that his career—a bright career at that—is with the Brooklyn Dodgers. We could discuss the matter further, but there's no real need to do so. Your brother's options are limited. He signs the contract and plays, or he doesn't sign and doesn't play."

On June 6, 1944, the same day the Cubs traded Eddie Stanky to Brooklyn, I signed the second contract with Rickey, this one attaching me to the major league Dodgers. I became a Dodger for life, or until they decided to dump me.

At 17, I had weighed 150 and was 6' even. Now at 18, I tipped the scales at 205 and stood 6'3". In a year, I'd gone from a boy to a man.

I was told to report to Ebbets Field, get my uniform, and suit up with the team. Brother Julie, eager to see what a big league clubhouse looked like, accompanied me. When we arrived at the ballpark, though, we saw a sign that said, GAME CANCELED. We didn't understand until we heard a kid waving a special edition of the *New York Daily News* and screaming, "Extra! Extra! Read all about it! Allied army lands in France! Great invasion under way!"

D-Day.

Teenage Rookie

I COULDN'T GET AWAY from the Polo Grounds.

One day I was there as a fan, rooting for the Giants against the Dodgers.

Two weeks later I was there as a Dodger, pitching against the Giants.

In the overnight transformation from fan to professional, a lifetime of love for the Giants flew out the window. All loyalty was transferred to the Dodgers. I suddenly disliked the Giants, the Cards, and the Phils. I especially disliked the Yankees. I related to the Dodgers, and the Dodgers alone. My entire household converted, along with my neighborhood. Mount Vernon became a distant suburb of Brooklyn. The Bums were once the enemy, but now we claimed them as our own. I identified, heart and soul, with the borough and its crazed baseball fans. I was born-again Brooklyn.

In 1944, the tide had turned against the Nazis. The rout was on. By October, the Japanese navy would be thoroughly defeated, and in November FDR would win a fourth term. Optimism was in the air.

In baseball, the story was St. Louis. The Cards met the St. Louis Browns for what they called a "Trolley Series" in Sportman's Park. Led by Musial—who'd hit .347 during the regular season with a slugging percentage of .522 during the Series—the Cards won, four games to two. That same year, my first with Brooklyn, we fell to eighth place and won only 63 games. The Cards won 105.

I spent most of the year warming the bench and spent the entire month of August in Montreal, the premier Dodger farm club. When I first arrived in the Brooklyn clubhouse—on June 7, 1944—the thing that shocked me most was the smoking. A lot of the Dodgers were smokers, *heavy* smokers. I thought baseball players, like me, modeled themselves on Jack Armstrong, All-American. I had a thing or two to learn about the real world.

During those first days I was intimidated. I remember watching big Hal Gregg, one of our aces. His '44 record was 9–16, but in '45 he'd win 18 games. His fastball probably clocked at 95 mph, but from my position on the bench it looked like 195 mph. How could I compete with that kind of speed? Who the hell did I think I was? Signing with the Dodgers was a fluke. Part of my mind was saying, *Branca, you don't deserve to be here.*

I was encouraged, though, when I saw other pitchers—guys even taller than I was—who lacked power. Johnny Gee, for example, who threw for the Giants, was a beast. He stood 6'9" and yet his fastball was so slow it wouldn't blacken your eye if it landed on your nose. As in basketball, extremely tall guys can lack coordination. Of course, in the 1990s, at 6'10", Randy Johnson, with more strikeouts per nine innings (10.67) than anyone, proved to be an exception.

During my rookie year, I spent a lot of time in the dugout sitting next to future Hall of Famer Paul Waner, the slugger they called Big Poison. In 1944 Waner was 41 years old, with his best years behind him. He'd been a major star for the Pirates, a three-time MVP who in 1926 had hit .380 and knocked in 131 runs. He was one of those Punch-and-Judy hitters who could slap a single in any direction. Waner wound up with a lifetime batting average of .333, no mean feat in any era. He had great stats. He also had whiskey breath—or at least something that smelled like booze. When the odor was too much for me, I moved down to the opposite end of the bench where, in my naive way, I asked Art Herring, a veteran pitcher, if it was possible that Waner drank.

"Did you hear what the kid asked?" Herring told a couple of the other old-timers sitting next to him. "He wants to know if it's *possible*—if it's *remotely possible*—that Big Poison might imbibe from time to time. What do you think, fellas?"

The fellas all laughed.

A week later Paul Waner and I were sleeping in twin beds at the Kenmore Hotel in Boston. Unlike today, where players demand private suites, everyone had a roommate. Waner and I were bunked up in close quarters.

I woke up first and was just about to get out of bed when I saw Waner open his eyes, reach under the bed, take out a bottle of booze, and pour it into a tumbler until it reached the top. He saw me looking at him.

"Orange juice," he said.

"Doesn't look like orange juice," I said.

"It's *my* orange juice, kid, and no one has to know that I drink it. Got it?"

"Got it."

After the Boston trip, on June 12, 1944, I made my major league debut. The ball park—as you've probably already guessed—was the Polo Grounds.

Once my incorruptible heroes, now my mortal enemies, the Giants were battering us 11–5 when I relieved in the bottom of the fourth. As I walked from the bullpen in deep center field I felt like I was on a treadmill. The walk went on and on. When I finally reached the mound, I quickly thought about all those years when

I had dreamed of this moment. My mother was in the stands, plus three of my brothers, even my aunt Rose. (A few weeks later Aunt Rose saw her first night game at Ebbets Field. When she called the experience "salubrious," I ran to the dictionary and learned that it meant healthful. With great confidence, I've been using the word ever since.)

Later I learned that my brother John was listening to the game at the Hendrix army base in Sebring, Florida, on the Armed Forces Radio Network. That's how he first found out that I had been signed by the Dodgers.

Even though my debut at Polo Grounds was during a lopsided game, I still wanted to shine. Pride required no less.

I was a fastball pitcher. That was my stock in trade. I didn't want to nibble around the corners and get behind in the count. I wanted to come at the hitters hard. And that's what I did. That day at the Polo Grounds my fastball was moving and, lo and behold, I struck out the first three men I faced. It helped, of course, that I was facing the bottom of the order.

An even bigger moment arrived the next inning, though, when I saw myself staring down at Mel Ott—my childhood idol. This couldn't be happening, but it was. Eighteen-year-old Ralph Branca was facing 35-year-old Mel Ott in his 19th season as a Giant. I swallowed hard. I stared in for the sign. A fastball on the inside. I pumped, wound, and delivered a perfect fastball on the inside. With his trademark motion, Mel lifted his right foot and swung, connecting a little late and lifting an easy pop fly to second base. I got him!

Other moments in my career would bring me a small degree of fame and a large degree of infamy. But no moment lives more vividly in my imagination as that inside fastball popped up by Mel Ott. Before I get carried away, though, I do have to add that in the fifth inning I served up a home run to Phil Weintraub, his second of the game. Before my career was over, I'd give up another 157 homers, but I'd also post an additional 826 strikeouts.

My big league pitching virginity may have been shattered with one swing of Weintraub's bat, but my personal virginity was intact. I'm not ashamed to admit that I clung to the principles set forth by my parents. *Don't fool around until you're really serious—and then wait until you're married.* My focus was on keeping hitters from scoring on me rather than trying to score on willing women.

I was introduced to the culture of big league baseball—and, specifically, the culture of the Brooklyn Dodgers—at a peculiar time. The war was still on and, in the case of the Dodgers, two of its biggest stars—Pee Wee Reese and Peter Reiser—were in the armed forces. At the start of the war, Commissioner Kenesaw Mountain Landis had asked Roosevelt about suspending play during the conflict. FDR replied with his famous "green light letter," stating that "Americans ought to have a chance for recreation and for taking their minds off work." He added that "night games [should] be extended because it gives an opportunity to the day shift to see a game." FDR thought like a fan.

The fan culture at Ebbets was wild. A woman named Hilda Chester had become almost as famous as the players. She was a lovable loudmouth who had something to say to everyone, especially the manager and coaches. She wore crazy flowered dresses and had a cowbell loud enough to drown out Miss Gladys Goodding's sweet organ playing "Take Me Out to the Ball Game." Sometimes Hilda waved a big sign that said, "Tell the World I'm From Brooklyn."

One time during a game I heard her screaming, "Branca! Branca!" I paid no attention. I was taught not to talk to the fans. "Ralph Branca, look at me when I'm talking to you!" she kept screaming. "Look at me! *For God's sake, it's me, Hilda!*" I looked at her and, with the authority of a schoolmarm, she handed me a note. "Give this to Durocher," she said. I walked over to the dugout and handed the note to Leo. He read it and made a pitching change. The reliever bombed and we lost the game.

Back in the clubhouse, I heard Leo say, "From now on, any time I get a note from Rickey, I'm gonna tear it up."

"It didn't come from Rickey," I said. "It came from Hilda."

"Why the hell didn't you tell me?" he barked.

"You didn't ask."

The atmosphere at Ebbets Field also featured the Dodger Symphony band, famous for playing "Three Blind Mice" when the umps made a bad call. The band was terrible but its leader, a cigar-smoking fan named Shorty Laurice, was irrepressible. In Ebbets Field, out-of-tune trombones and tubas were just what the doctor ordered.

Visually, of course, Ebbets was also a mess. That added to its lovability. The big Schaefer beer scoreboard in right field had the "h" and first "e" outlined in neon. At the right moment, "h" for "hit" or "e" for "error" would light up, in those days a technological marvel. Beneath the scoreboard an ad read, "HIT SIGN WIN SUIT. ABE STARK." Stark was a guy selling suits on Pitkin Avenue. On that same curved wall were billboards for Gem razors, Bulova watches, Old Gold cigarettes, and Esquire boot polish. At Ebbets Field nothing matched, yet everything came together beautifully.

When I arrived that fateful day in June, I was given a uniform with number 13 on the back. It had belonged to Kirby Higbe, a good pitcher who'd won 22 games in 1941 and was now in the armed services.

"Any objections?" asked equipment manager Dan Camerford.

"None," I said.

"That's odd," said Dan. "Most guys think it's bad luck."

"I'm not most guys," I said. "I'm a contrarian. It goes with my nature. Matter of fact, if you'd given me my choice, I'd pick number 13."

"Well then, this is your lucky day, Mr. Contrarian. Wear it well."

"I will."

•

In my era the logistics of baseball were basic. There were only 10 major league cities—three teams in New York; two in St. Louis, Chicago, Boston, and Philly; and one in Cincy, Pittsburgh, Detroit, Cleveland, and D.C. Each league had only eight teams: Dodgers, Giants, Cards, Cubs, Braves, Phillies, Pirates, and Reds in the National; and Yanks, Browns, Tigers, Red Sox, White Sox, Indians, Senators, and A's in the American.

Win the pennant and play in the World Series. No playoffs. Missouri was as far west as you went. And, of course, you went everywhere on the train. The Dodgers had three train cars of their own. The press came along. Dick Young, the first of the poison pen men, was a hand-me-down from the Giants. His reports in the *New York Daily News* were too negative for Giant owner Horace Stoneham. In those days the owners could nix the reporters. Someone once said Young's style had the subtlety of "a kick in the nuts."

One time Young wrote that our left fielder, Gene Hermanski, played a base hit like "a charging clown." The next day Hermanski grabbed Young by the throat. It took two of us to restrain Gene and save Young's life. A few of the Dodgers weren't sure it was worth saving. In a previous era, when Babe Ruth was cavorting, scandalous material wasn't deemed appropriate to print. The media protected you. Young turned that around. He went after you. His attitude would have been easier to take had we not known that Young, who sat in his hotel room with binoculars aimed at women's bedrooms, was a notorious skirt chaser.

The train trips, on the Pennsylvania Railroad or New York Central, were tedious. St. Louis was 27 hours. Some of the Dodgers were card sharks. They liked gin and hearts and especially poker. I was scared of poker, so I stayed away. My aim was to save enough money to help buy my folks a better house in Mount Vernon. I was conservative, even as a young teen.

I was given a nickname by Dixie Walker, our captain and right fielder. He christened me "Hawk" because of my big nose. How could I argue with a guy like Dixie, especially in 1944, when he led the league hitting .357? Besides, Hawks are tough. The Dodgers were tough, but also welcoming. They were also ethnically diverse, a fact that, given my League of Nations upbringing in Mount Vernon, made me comfortable. Luis Olmo, for example, an outfielder who came to Brooklyn in '43, was one of the first Puerto Ricans in the majors. He was also the first man to employ the basket catch, later made famous by Willie Mays.

I wasn't getting much action in '44, but I was getting used to a big league culture that was light-years away from what it is today. After a game at Ebbets Field, for example, I'd shower, dress, and head for the subway station for the long trek back to Mount Vernon. Sometimes kids would be waiting for me. They'd walk me to the subway and several would actually ride the train with me through Brooklyn, Manhattan, and the Bronx. They were young teenagers—12, maybe 13 years old—and of course I was still a teenager myself. They'd ask questions about the game. How do you pitch Stan Musial as opposed to Mel Ott? How do you throw a slider? What's it like to be on the same team as Dixie Walker? I loved talking to these kids. I enjoyed their company. It was only a few years before that I was their age, dreaming the same dreams dancing through their heads. This was a time when players were approachable and actually moved and worked among the fans.

In August, just when I was adjusting to my new life, Rickey shipped me to Montreal. He said I needed some additional seasoning, but not to worry, I'd be back. The AAA farm team was managed by an old-timer, Bruno Betzel, who basically did Branch's bidding. Rickey also had theories he wanted to test—and the players, of course, were the guinea pigs.

He postulated that pitchers were being underused. If pitchers could throw more often, he'd need fewer of them. Costs would drop and profits would rise. Rickey had been a catcher and, to my way of thinking, lacked a fundamental respect for pitchers. Many jocks, me included, will argue that pitching is the toughest job in all sports. The human arm is simply not meant to be exerted to this extreme degree. Without great care, you can permanently damage yourself in no time flat. Back in the 1940s, the term "sports medicine" did not exist. When it came to training, it was the Dark Ages. Branch Rickey came out of the Dark Ages with this notion that pitchers could start every third day. That meant two days rest. Because I was young and strong, he decided to experiment on me. I was powerless to argue and went along with the plan—and nearly threw my arm out. In a month, I started 11 games and pitched 71 innings.

By September I was back with Brooklyn, warming the bench once again while we fought the Phils to avoid the basement.

"You did all right up in Montreal," Rickey said when I returned. "You pitched with very little rest."

"I'd have pitched better with more rest."

"That's what all the pitchers say."

"I don't mean to be impudent, Mr. Rickey, but those pitchers are right."

The Lip

L EO DUROCHER GETS to lead off a chapter of his own.

Not only is he one of the most charismatic characters in sports history, he's also key to my personal history. He was my first major league manager and the first important baseball man to recognize my potential firsthand.

Leo was a pool-hustlin' dead-end kid from West Springfield, Massachusetts, a poor town west of Boston where he could literally watch the noxious gashouse fumes floating over the Connecticut River. He was never a great hitter but had good hands as a shortstop. For my money, his managing acumen is up there with the best—John McGraw, Connie Mack, Casey Stengel, Tony LaRussa, Bobby Cox, and my son-in-law, Bobby Valentine.

Leo was tough, but Leo was brilliant. I'd sit at his end of the dugout and hear him talk to his coaches. He was five steps ahead of the opposing manager. He was an anticipator, a chess player, a strategist of uncommon skill. Mostly, though, he hated to lose.

Our relationship was cemented during spring training when we were playing the Yankees. Johnny Lindell—soon to gain notoriety for hitting .500 against us in the '47 World Series—was an aggressive base runner. Nothing wrong with that, except that an exhibition game is not the time to endanger an opponent. So when Lindell stormed into second base spikes high, Durocher was furious.

In the dugout, Leo said to me, "That guy has no goddamn right to go after one of our guys when it doesn't even count. I'm putting you in there, Branca, 'cause next time he comes up I wanna see him on his ass."

There are a lot of ways to go after a hitter. If you want to hurt a guy, you stick it in his ribs or go for a knee. That wasn't my style. I didn't mind knocking guys down—there were times when I liked it—but I viewed the knockdown pitch as an art. A perfectly placed pitch to his chin and you'll see him fall. In the case of Lindell, I put one right between his shoulder blades. He didn't have time to get out of the way and wound up on the ground. Never have I seen Leo so happy. The guys sitting next to him claimed he had an orgasm.

"That's it, Branca!" he said after the inning was over. "That's the way to show those bastards we mean business."

It's been said that Durocher would knock down his own mother to steal second base.

"I would," he once admitted to me, "but not during spring training. Only during the regular season."

Leo's favorite expression when I faced a hitter requiring a brush-back was, "Stick it in his ear!"

Durocher was a tremendous competitor whose coarse language became his trademark. His mother, your mother, no one's mother was exempt from Leo's linguistic arsenal. He was a vulgarian but not a racist. He'd curse any ethnic group, but, in his mind, with fondness. In his autobiography *Nice Guys Finish Last*, he remembered that Joe D referred to himself as "Big Dago" and Phil Rizzuto as "Little Dago." "For as long as I've been in baseball," Durocher wrote, "every Italian has been called a Dago and every Jew a Hebe. Given a certain inflection, it can be a sign of affection."

I liked Leo because he liked me. Later in his checkered career, after he was fired from the Dodgers and hired by the Giants, he wanted to trade for me. He offered up Bobby Thomson. Brooklyn wouldn't budge, though. If they had, I probably wouldn't be writing this book.

When Dodger managers such as Charlie Dressen, Burt Shotton, and Walter Alston could be doddering and dull as dishwater, Durocher was dynamite. He exploded on a regular basis—at players, at his general manager, and especially at umpires. I related. I liked having a fiery manager, especially one who marked his strategy with exceptional shrewdness. I liked that he fought with Branch Rickey, a man who plotted to control every aspect of the Dodger universe.

Leo was no one's fool, or tool. Independence was his middle name. It warmed my heart that he appreciated pitchers not afraid to brush back hitters who had, in one form or another, dealt unkindly with the pitchers' teammates. He was also anything but wishy-washy; once he decided on a course of action, that was it. He tended to intimidate his minions—chief among them, coach Charlie Dressen—and that, you will soon see, had a major effect on the vicious Dodger-Giant rivalry.

Leo loved the limelight. He was a natty dresser who all but begged the photographers to take his picture when he dined at Sardi's with Walter Winchell or hung at Jack Dempsey's Broadway Restaurant on Times Square with Frank Sinatra. He liked Broadway characters because he himself was one. He liked politicians, pop singers, and movie stars, and wasn't shy about shaking hands with more than a few famous shady figures. He had a flashy smile and was one of the first managers to become a media superstar. (Later in his life he appeared in an ad for Jockey Color Underwear saying, "I wear 'em and I'm as much of a man as you are!")

I was not privy to the front office explosions between Durocher and Rickey. The men were incompatible, opposites in nearly every way. Rickey was a Bible thumper, Durocher a gambler; Rickey spoke the King's English, Durocher swore like a sailor. Rickey was a skinflint, Durocher a spendthrift. Leo described Branch as the "great man in my life." He also said that Rickey operated the Cardinals in the 1930s like a "chain gang." Leo liked to speculate that Rickey could have been elected governor of Missouri and, in his memoir, added, "We'd have been perfectly safe if he had been running the country." For all the animosity between these two titans, there also was respect.

Rickey held on to Durocher because he saw him as a winner. But he deplored Leo's freewheeling lifestyle. Rickey felt everyone should marry and encouraged his players to do so, the sooner the better. The way Rickey saw it, marriage—especially for athletic young men—was essential for moral integrity.

When Leo got married the second time, in 1934, Rickey was overjoyed. But the marriage didn't last, and neither did two others. Leo liked his ladies; he liked high-stakes card games, and he liked the track. Off the field he liked looking like a million bucks and once told Rickey, "You could pay a thousand dollars for a suit and in twenty minutes you'd look like you fell out of bed."

At the end of our dismal 1944 season, Durocher sent me home with the admonition to stay in shape. He had nothing to worry about. In the off-season I continued to study at NYU and revved up my basketball game. I started an amateur team called the Branca All-Stars that included fellow NYU student Eddie Yost, who'd been signed by the Washington Senators for third base. Eddie would be known as the Walking Man for his ability to draw bases on balls. He was a great leadoff man. He also played a tough point guard. One of the only times I got into a no-holds-barred brawl involved Eddie. We were playing basketball at the Mount Vernon Armory. I had the ball and saw Eddie had an open lane. I shot him a crosscourt pass and watched him charge the basket for what should have been an easy layup. As he went up, though, the defender attacked him from behind, and Eddie went crashing to the floor. Luckily, he was only bruised. If he'd fallen in a slightly different direction, though, he might have suffered a career-ending injury, as his career was just getting started.

When the assault happened, I saw red. I raced over, jumped on Eddie's attacker, and started punching him in the face. He fought back, but not before I landed enough blows to give him the lesson he deserved.

That off-season I also was able to help buy my folks a better home in Mount Vernon, at 409 Seneca Avenue. My salary for the season was $3,300, about the same price as the house itself. Naturally, I continued to live with my family—and would do so for as long as I was single.

During those cold winter mornings I'd get up early to study before class and read the papers. In December came the shocking news that the beloved bandleader Glenn Miller was thought to be dead. His plane had gone down in the English Channel. Miller had been playing for the troops, and his songs, such as "Moonlight Serenade," "String of Pearls," and "In the Mood," had provided the background of our lives.

I continually worried for the safety of my brothers. I knew Mom worried as well, but, a strong woman, she kept the faith. Every morning before my long trek to college, she'd fix my breakfast. I'd just turned 19. In that first year with the Dodgers I'd seen something of the country, but I was still wet behind the ears. Mom knew that. She also knew that, in spite of having earned a spot in the major leagues, I felt pangs of guilt for not serving the country.

By January 1945, the Russians had taken Warsaw. The Nazis were crumbling.

"I know you want to fight," said Mom, "but you are fighting. You're fighting for the honor of your family and your country when you go out there and play baseball."

"That's not the same thing, Mom," I said. "It's just a game."

"It's a game that you play with all your heart, Ralphie. The way you play makes us all proud. You give us all hope, son. You keep our spirits high, and there's no greater gift than that. I know you want to be a soldier, but the truth is that you are. When you put on that Dodger uniform and go out there and win, you're a soldier as brave as any of your brothers."

Mom's words made a difference. With renewed vigor, I went to Dodgers spring training at Bear Mountain, near West Point. That was the winter I met Jim and Dearie Mulvey, their daughters Ann and Marie, and son Buddy. Dearie Mulvey was the only child of Steve McKeever who, along with his brother, owned the construction company that had built Ebbets Field. Strapped for cash, Charlie Ebbets paid them in equity, giving McKeever and his brother each 25 percent of the ballpark. Eventually each brother also received 25 percent of the Dodgers. Steve McKeever died a young man, leaving his daughter Dearie his share of the team.

They were great people and enthusiastic Dodger fans, a family who loved baseball as much as the Brancas. For all their social status, they weren't the least bit stuck up. When they showed up at spring training, they arrived as fans and were friendly with everyone. The Mulvey who really caught my attention, I must admit, was their beautiful daughter Ann.

In March, General Patton's Third Army crossed the Rhine while the Dodgers, under General Durocher, were preparing an assault on the National League. Big stars such as Pee Wee Reese, Pete Reiser, and Hugh Casey were still in the armed services, but Durocher, always the optimist, was predicting a pennant for Brooklyn, its first since '41.

"You're a big part of our operation," Leo told me in early April.

On April 13, 1945, just as our First, Third, and Ninth armies were about to take Berlin, President Roosevelt died of a cerebral hemorrhage. Harry Truman became our 32nd president.

On April 17, we opened the season at Ebbets Field against the Phils. Durocher, our manager/player at second base, had two RBIs. We won 8–2. I couldn't have been happier.

On April 18, I couldn't have been unhappier. Leo called me into his office and said, "You know, I was the one responsible for getting skinflint Rickey to give you a raise to $450 a month."

"And I appreciate it," I said.

"Damn good pay for a 19-year-old kid."

"Pretty good," I answered. I thought I was worth more.

"It'll get better. Especially after you get back from Minnesota."

"What's in Minnesota?"

"The Dodgers' Triple-A farm team. The St. Paul Saints."

"I already put in my time in Montreal."

"The Saints need help and you could use a little more seasoning."

"In Montreal, Rickey gave me so much seasoning I nearly threw my arm out."

"Don't worry about Rickey," said Durocher. "That two-day-rest experiment is over."

"I pictured myself pitching in the majors all season," I said.

"Keep that picture in your head, kid. It's gonna come true."

When a reporter got on Durocher's case for sending one of his better pitching prospects to the minors, he shot back, "I can recall Branca any minute if I want him. He's going to be a major league pitcher—no doubt about that."

I shipped off to Minnesota and, as a Saint, struck out 94 in 100 innings. My record was 6–5 and my ERA 3.33. The Dodgers called me back to Brooklyn in July.

We were playing the Cubs on July 18 at Wrigley Field when I returned to the team. We were in the middle of a hot pennant race, half a game behind the Cards and just three and a half behind the league-leading Cubbies.

Chicago shut us out in the first game of the Wednesday afternoon doubleheader, 5–0. In the second game, we were winning 7–5, but the Cubs had rallied and loaded the bases. With two out,

Phil Cavaretta came to bat. Durocher walked to the mound and asked pitcher Tom Seats for the ball. Then he signaled to the bullpen. "Bring in Branca."

I was ready to roll. After my warm-up pitches, I steeled myself, took a deep breath, and got down to business. I looked in at the sign. The catcher called for heat, high inside. I got it where I wanted it. Phil Cavaretta popped out, and we went on to win the game.

"Thatta boy, Branca," said Leo when I got to the dugout. "Consider yourself a big league starter."

Starter or not, I secured myself my first big league save. I was stoked.

The Dodgers collapsed in late summer, finishing the season third behind the Cards and the pennant-winning Cubs, who got beaten by Detroit four games to three in the World Series. That was the last time the Cubs made the Series, at least through 2010. I wish them well in 2011. Back in the last half of '45, I threw seven complete games in 15 starts with an ERA of 3.04. My record was 5–6 but should have been 9–2.

Pitchers complain. Pitchers give excuses. I'm a pitcher and, no doubt, I'm prone to complaining and giving excuses. I don't apologize for this. It's an occupational hazard. To a large degree, it's also a phenomenon based on fact. And in 1945, the fact is that a player named Tommy Brown cost me at least four games. Brown was the only Dodger I distinctly disliked.

Brown was a shortstop who came up with me in '44. In '45, at age 17, he became the youngest major leaguer ever to hit a homer, his one great distinction. Tommy was deeply in love with himself. He was convinced he was the next Joe D, even to the point of copying DiMaggio's batting stance.

I knew Joe D.

Joe D was a friend of mine.

Tommy B was no Joe D.

Tommy would come to batting practice early and have the neighborhood kids pitch to him. He'd keep a running count of how many batting practice homers he hit. He claimed they were in the hundreds. In truth, though, he was a mediocre hitter and a lousy fielder. I'd've been better off with a totem pole standing out there at shortstop. Tommy's one outstanding attribute was his strong arm.

The summer of 1945 was a pivotal one for the world. Germany surrendered in May, and by July the Japanese navy was in shambles. On August 6 and 9, atomic bombs were dropped on Hiroshima and Nagasaki. Five days later Emperor Hirohito surrendered to General MacArthur.

My brothers survived the war, and the Branca family had much to be grateful for.

On August 14, the day after the big war ended, I was pitching a 1–0 one-hit shutout against the Cards in Ebbets Field. In the top of the sixth Tommy Brown fielded a grounder at shortstop. It should have been a routine out. Brown threw the ball 20 feet over first base. The result was a run that tied the game.

In the top of the ninth of this same game, I was locked in a 1–1 pitcher's duel with St. Louis' ace Harry Brecheen. He'd given up five hits; I'd given up two. With two out, I faced Whitey Kurowski. I was behind in the count, 3–1. Here's where my third-base coach, Charlie Dressen, flaunted his ineptitude. Despite being tutored by Durocher, Charlie was not a cunning strategist. The fact that he operated for most of his early career in Leo's shadow would later have a deleterious effect on the Dodgers—and me.

So I was looking in for my sign on this 3–1 pitch when, from the dugout, I heard this ear-splitting whistle emanating from Charlie's mouth. The world knew that this meant curveball. Charlie's whistle had always meant curveball. Rather than telegraph the pitch, why not trot out to the mound and whisper, "Throw a curve!"? Or just let the catcher do his job and give me the sign himself? That wasn't Charlie. Charlie wanted the curve so Charlie whistled for the curve.

Young Ralph Branca, a 19-year-old eager to please his manager and coach so that he could remain a starter, threw the curve. Knowing what was coming, Kurowski readied himself and drove the ball into the seats in deep left-center. We lost 2–1.

It feels good to air my complaints about poor fielding and an imprudent coach. I should admit that I didn't have to face Stan Musial in this game I pitched so well. Musial spent 1945 in the navy. When he returned in 1946, he hit .365 and won the MVP. That was the year he was dubbed "The Man." It happened at Ebbets Field, where he terrorized our team. During one streak there, he went 11 for 14. The Dodger fans, loyal as they were, knew talent when they saw it. They gave Stan his due. They gave him standing ovations. Every time he came to the plate they chanted "The Man" in recognition of his athletic genius. Stan hit the ball where it was pitched. He almost never overswung, and yet he slugged an average of 25 home runs a season. One of my favorite stats is not only Stan's lifetime average—.331—but his total hits of 3,630, divided exactly evenly between 1,815 at home and 1,815 on the road. In 1948, the year he hit his career-best .376, I asked my fellow pitcher Preacher Roe, "How the hell can you ever get this guy out?"

"I walk him," said Preacher, "and when he's tapping his foot on first, I pick him off between taps."

El Cheapo

HAPPY DAYS WERE here again. The war was over. The war was won.

When I went off with the Dodgers on the USO tour of the Pacific in the winter of 1945, I was elated. It was my first time on a plane, my first time out of the country, and my only taste of the military. We played army and navy teams on their bases in Guam, Hawaii, and the Philippines. It was sobering to see the shrapnel and bullet holes in the stadiums. The soldiers greeted us like heroes, even though they were the ones who'd done the fighting. The games were spirited—there was lots of baseball talent in the armed services—and we had great fun.

I got home in January. I knew it was going to be a good year. The country was at peace and the Dodgers, helped by my strong finish in '45, had recognized my talent. Or had they?

When I got off the plane in San Francisco, I called Mount Vernon to check on my parents. My brother Paul answered the phone.

"Mom and Dad are fine," he said. "And you just got a letter from the Dodgers."

"Open it, Paul."

"It's your contract for next season."

"And no letter of explanation?"

"None."

"How much is it for?"

"It says three thousand three hundred."

"That's what I made last year. Are you sure?"

"It's right in front of me, Ralph. Same salary. No raise."

"That's bullshit," I said.

"Are you going to sign?"

"Hell, no."

I flew back home in a rage. I knew I was worth more. But remember—in those days, players had no representative, no agent, no lawyer. Nothing.

Branch Rickey, who had run a chain gang in St. Louis, was running the Dodgers the same way. He was exploiting me because I was young. I also resented how he sent a contract with neither explanation nor a chance to respond. Were there to be no negotiations? Had I nothing to say in the matter?

Soon as I got home, I went down to 215 Montague Street to see Rickey—but he wouldn't see me. All I could do was leave my request with his secretary. I wanted a $2,700 raise that would bring my salary to $6,000, hardly an unreasonable request.

"What will you do if he doesn't give it to you?" asked Paul that night.

"He'll give it to me."

"And if he don't?"

"I'll boycott spring training until he caves."

"How will you get in shape?"

"I'll work out on my own."

With the Dodgers in Florida, I went back to NYU to study during the day. At night I worked out at the Mount Vernon YMCA. A couple of reporters came looking for me.

"Why aren't you with the club?" they asked.

I answered honestly. "Because Rickey is too cheap to pay me what I'm worth."

Next thing I knew, the *New York Daily News* was calling Branch Rickey "El Cheapo."

Later I was asked if I was the one who gave Rickey the El Cheapo label.

"I didn't give him anything," I said. "He earned it."

During my holdout, a reporter from the *Brooklyn Eagle* asked, "How long are you going to boycott?"

"Long as I have to."

Employing the insensitive racial terminology of the day, Jimmy Powers, a well-known sports journalist, wrote, "Branch Rickey paid Branca, his white starting pitcher, less money than a colored bus boy collects each week in the lowliest Miami hotel."

I held out all of February. I wasn't going to budge. I had my principles.

But on March 12, I compromised my principles. I couldn't stand the idea of the Dodgers down in spring training with me twiddling my thumbs in Mount Vernon. I went to Grand Central and bought a ticket with my own money for Daytona Beach. When I got there, Durocher was happy to see me but Rickey was cool. He let me stew for several days before he agreed to see me.

"You've gone to the press," he said.

"The press came to me," I explained.

"They didn't force you to talk."

"No, sir. But you did. You shut down communications between us. You wouldn't listen to me, but at least the press would. You sent me a contract without explanation."

"You're a 20-year-old. What explanation do you think you are owed?"

"A reasonable one."

"Here's your reasonable contract. Sign it." He shoved it in front of me. The salary still said $3,300.

"I don't think $3,300 is reasonable."

"And what do you think is a reasonable salary?"

I ran off my stats from last year and then added, "And they'd be a lot better if Tommy Brown knew how to catch or throw a ball."

"Let's get down to brass tacks, Branca," Rickey replied. "How much do you want?"

"Six thousand."

He answered, "No young player in your age bracket is making that kind of money."

When you're 20 years old, and you've never been in a real negotiation, you don't have an answer. I knew that another young player was making $6,500, but I couldn't reveal that I knew that. Rickey flat out lied to me. He wanted to keep my salary down as long as possible, because he knew he'd eventually have to pay me much more.

Rickey said, "Take five and consider yourself lucky."

I took the five.

Word got around training camp that I had shook down Rickey. Naturally, I was excited to be back with my team—doubly excited because this was the year, 1946, when Cookie Lavagetto, Pee Wee Reese, Peter Reiser, and Hugh Casey were back from the war. Before he left in 1942, Casey's ERA was 2.25. Reiser was a superb hitter and fielder, a guy who was ready—and even eager—to sacrifice every bone in his body to make a catch. He was famous for crashing into the unpadded left- and center-field walls of Ebbets Field. He'd make circus catches during batting practice.

We were also encouraged by the arrival of a hard-nosed player from Reading, Pennsylvania—Carl Furillo, who would become the most celebrated right fielder in the history of Ebbets Field. Before Carl retired, he'd hit over .300 five times and be forever known as the Reading Rifle. His arm was remarkable. Woe to any hitter looking to take an extra base off Carl. When it came to nailing runners, Carl was deadly. From great distances, he could throw the ball into a teacup.

Pee Wee was our captain. In 16 distinguished seasons with the Dodgers, he was the steady beating heart of the team. When it came to leadership, Pee Wee was a natural. He led with a calm demeanor. He kept a lid on things. He didn't shout or scold, but spoke softly, motivating us with his own brand of steely determination. In that sense, Reese was a perfect counterpoint to Durocher. From the dugout, Leo energized us with his stomping and screaming. On the field, Pee Wee calmed us with his unflappability. He was a gentleman from Louisville, Kentucky. There were flashier players, but none more beloved or respected by their teammates.

So when, just before the '46 season started, Pee Wee suggested that I replace him as team rep, I was floored. To this day I'm not sure why he picked me. It may be because I was a college kid, or because he liked the way I had challenged Rickey. Either way, I became his guy. When he suggested that the Dodgers elect me, they did so unanimously.

In the pre–player-union era, the job meant very little, but I was honored nonetheless. We were not allowed to address issues of any substance—such as salary negotiations or, God forbid, the reserve clause. The only thing I can remember accomplishing is convincing the Cubs to install a bathroom on the first floor near the visitors' dugout. The only other facility was on the third floor and sometimes, in a short half inning, we wouldn't have time to do our business and get back out on the field.

We began the season on April 16 against Boston at Braves Field. Kirby Higbe, back from the war, reclaimed his number 13 and I was given number 20. I loved 13, but Higbe was a very good starting pitcher, so I had to respect his wishes.

We split that opening series in Boston and took the train back to New York, where we trounced the Giants 8–1 in Ebbets Field on April 18. We were off to a good start. In '46 we won eight of our first nine games. I remember we had an off-day on April 19 because I spent the morning in Mount Vernon reading the paper.

Naturally, I read the sports section. I was going over the box score of how we beat the Giants when an item caught my eye.

The Dodger AAA club the Montreal Royals had opened the season at Roosevelt Stadium in Jersey City against the Giants' Class AAA International League farm team, also named the Giants. More than 50,000 people were there, an amazing number, especially considering that 18,000 fewer fans had come to see us take on the Giants the day before. As I read on, the reason became clear: Montreal was starting a second baseman named Jackie Robinson. In the modern era, no black man had ever played pro ball outside the Negro Leagues before. Robinson's debut was spectacular—a home run, three singles, two stolen bases, three RBIs, four runs scored. Montreal won 14–1. Robinson would go on to lead the Royals to victory in what was called the Little World Series. I wondered whether Rickey was thinking of bringing him up to the Dodgers. I hoped so. Southerners on our team would resist, but I couldn't have cared less. I knew Robinson would help us win. He sounded like my kind of competitor, and that's all that mattered.

I had a hard time getting going in '46. Maybe it was because of my late arrival in spring training, but whatever the reason, I was frustrated. I made my first appearance on April 22, against the Braves in Ebbets Field. My family was in the stands and I wanted to shine. After all, this was my first year as a certified starter.

In the second inning Whitey Wietelmann blasted a line drive right at me. It caught my right elbow and stung something fierce. I was sore, but didn't say a word to the trainer back in the dugout. I wanted a complete game, and I wanted a win. I struggled through seven innings, giving up four runs and seven hits, when I got the ol' heave-ho. We came back and won 5–4 in the tenth, and Hugh Casey got the victory in relief.

My elbow injury nagged and I couldn't throw for a few days. Leo decided to bench me for a while, and I hated missing the time.

"Don't worry, Ralph," said Charlie Dressen. "You can pitch batting practice."

No starter wants to pitch batting practice, especially after he's worked his ass off to make the rotation. But I did what I was told. When he asked a third or fourth time, though, I got ticked off.

"You can't make any friggin' money throwing batting practice," I said in disgust.

Dressen didn't appreciate the comment. He turned away from me and didn't talk to me for a month. He didn't like a player giving him attitude. At the time, I didn't care. I wanted to start. In my eagerness, though, I succeeded in alienating Leo's first lieutenant. Dumb politics. But what do you expect from a brash 20-year-old looking to prove himself?

As the season plodded on, I was getting little or no action. The daily traipse to Ebbets Field was getting to me. I'd walk the four blocks from our house to catch the bus that took me to 241st Street and White Plains Road in the Bronx. The other riders—the workers, the school kids, the housewives—seemed cheerful compared to me. I'd take the Lexington Avenue subway to Grand Central, then the shuttle to Times Square, where all the hustle and bustle of midtown Manhattan still didn't lift my spirits. On the long BMT ride to Brooklyn, my mood wouldn't lighten. I'd get off at the Prospect Park station and walk over to the ballpark, all the time thinking, *I began the season as a starter. Now, at best, I'm being used in relief. Mostly, though, I'm just pitching batting practice. Isn't that how I started off with the Dodgers when I was 16? In four years, I haven't made any progress. I'm getting nowhere fast.*

Those were the depressing thoughts assaulting my mind as I sat in front of my locker in the clubhouse. My head was down, my body limp. I was feeling hopeless.

"What's wrong, kid?" asked Augie Galan, a veteran outfielder who, in spite of having a strong year at the plate, wasn't getting as much play as rookie Carl Furillo. Augie, though, was Mr. Positive. He had a good word for everyone.

"Dressen has me in the doghouse," I said.

"Dressen ain't running this team. Durocher is. And Durocher likes you."

"Maybe," I countered, "but he listens to Dressen, and Dressen has me picking daisies in the bullpen."

"Gonna tell you something, Ralphie, and I want you to listen," Augie said as he put his arm around my shoulder. "You're going through the same shit every player goes through. This game runs in cycles. You got your high cycles and you got your low cycles. You're in a low cycle right now, but sure as I'm standing here, that's going to change. I guaran-goddamn-tee you."

"How can you be so sure, Augie?" I asked.

"Because I've seen you pitch. You got the goods, son, and soon the world's gonna know about it."

Coming from an older guy with heart, that pep talk helped. It's no accident that a month later I experienced my turning point as a major leaguer. It happened in September during a torrid pennant fight with the Cardinals.

With two weeks left in the season, St. Louis was coming to Ebbets Field for a crucial three-game series. They won Thursday's game, but we came back to win on Friday, putting us only a game and a half behind in the race for first place. The Saturday game, the rubber match, was critical. If we lost, we'd fall back two and a half games; if we won, we'd be only half a game out.

Dressen still wasn't giving me any love. He barely talked to me. So when Durocher approached me in the clubhouse, I took heart. Maybe Durocher still believed in me.

"Ralphie," he said, "I'm starting you today."

My heart started racing. "That's great, Leo! I know this is an important game and I won't let you down."

"Don't worry about that. There won't be time to let me down."

"What are you talking about?"

"I'm talking about using you as a decoy. If I list you as my starter, the Cards will load up their lineup with lefthanders. After the first hitter, I'll take you out and bring in Lombardi."

Vic Lombardi, one of our aces, threw left-handed. I threw right.

"So I'm your sacrificial lamb?" I asked.

"Something like that—yeah."

I didn't like the plan. I hated it. As I warmed up, I got angrier and angrier. With each pitch, I got more steamed up. *Sacrificial lamb, my ass!* I kept saying to myself.

The Card lineup was formidable. The first three hitters were Red Schoendienst, Harry Walker, and Stan Musial. It took me a total of five pitches to get them out in order.

When I reached the dugout, Leo was all grins.

"You don't want to be yanked, do you, kid?"

"Hell, no!" I said.

"Well, keep throwing like that and I'll keep you in."

On that day, September 14, 1946, I felt like I earned my stripes as a big league pitcher. I shut out the Cardinals 5–0, striking out nine while allowing two walks and three hits—singles by Walker, Musial, and Joe Garagiola. Five days later, in my next appearance, I shut out the Pirates 3–0. I made my point.

Durocher got the point, and by the end of the regular season, in a breathtaking tooth-and-nail battle, we had caught the Cards. For the first time in major league history, a three-game playoff series was being held to decide the pennant. Two questions remained: Where were the games to be held, and who would pitch?

The first question was decided by the toss of a coin. Brooklyn won. Rickey's—or Durocher's—decision came down to this: You can open at home and play the next two on the road. Or you can open on the road and play the next two at home. The Dodgers decided to take the 27-hour train trip to St. Louis. And Durocher decided to start me.

I was elated and not all that surprised. After all, just two weeks before I had shut out this Cardinal team. Leo knew that I wasn't afraid to pitch the big game. Hell, I was eager to pitch the big game.

After we failed to score in the top of the first, I took the mound that Tuesday, October 1, 1946, in Sportsman's Park with all the confidence in the world. I got leadoff man Red Schoendienst on called strikes. I missed on a curveball to Terry Moore, who singled. But then I found my stride with Musial, who went down looking. Their cleanup man, Enos Slaughter, singled weakly between first and second. I was too careful with Whitey Kurowski and walked him, loading the bases with two out. My confidence had not left me. My pitches were moving up and down, in and out, and I felt in control. I just needed to get their rookie catcher, Joe Garagiola, and I'd be out of the inning.

I fooled Joe on the first two pitches, but when I tried to jam him inside he hit a soft line drive over my head. Moore scored from third. Bases still loaded. I wasn't shook. I was convinced that I'd get out of this inning. And when I got Harry Walker on a roller that forced Garagiola at second, I did. Two fluke hits, one run, three left on base. I felt like I dodged a bullet.

I sailed through the second—three up, three down.

Howie Schultz hit the first pitch of the third inning into the left-field seats. Dodgers 1, Cards 1.

In the bottom of the third, Terry Moore hit a lazy fly to right. Easy out for Furillo. Now here comes Musial. I pitched him cautiously—maybe too cautiously—and he drew a walk. Then Slaughter singled to right and Musial took third. Two on, one out. Kurowski hit a slow grounder that drove in Musial while Slaughter was forced out at second. Garagiola at the plate. This time Joe hit another dying liner, this one barely to the center-field grass, about 143 feet. Everyone was safe. Bases loaded, two out. Another moment of pressure. But, in my mind, another moment to shine. Determined to get out of the jam, I faced Harry Walker. My pitches still had good movement, and I fooled him on an inside fastball. But like Garagiola in the first, Harry got on top of the ball; his Baltimore chop was a mile high and landed behind the mound. Whitey scored from third. The Cards were up 3–1, on lucky hits. I was certain I still had my stuff.

Leo was not certain. He pulled me for Kirby Higbe. By the time the game was over, each team managed another run and the Cards won 4–2. After an interminable train ride back to the East Coast, the Cards also won the second game, at Ebbets Field, 8–4, and went on to beat the Red Sox in a thrilling 4–3 World Series.

At season's end, I was proud to have been one of two starting pitchers in the first play-off game ever. At 20 I was also the youngest to ever start a postseason game, a record that still stands.

At the same time, the play-off loss was tough. In three innings I'd given up six singles, four of which were flukes. My strength and accuracy were intact. I had weathered one storm in the first and knew I could weather another in the third. I was about to do just that when Leo pulled me. Do I blame him? Hell, yes.

I blame him in the name of all pitchers who blame their managers for lacking confidence in them. I blame him in the name of all cocky young jocks hungry for just a little more time to prove themselves. I blame him because, as an old-timer looking back at my days as a youngblood, I can't help but believe I would have gotten out of the inning. Finally, though, I blame him because, if you're going to tell baseball stories and indulge in second-guessing, the blame game is part of the fun.

Which brings me to 1947—the year I had the most fun of all.

The Year That Changed
the World

D ON'T BE MISLED by the title of this chapter. Yes, I won 21 games in 1947; and yes, I led the league in starts with 36. I had the third-best ERA: 2.67, behind Ewell Blackwell (2.47) and Warren Spahn (2.33). Blackwell led the league with strikeouts (193), and I was second (148). I pitched 280 innings, gave up 251 hits, and walked 98. I never missed a single start. My salary was $6,500, and I still took the bus and two subways to work.

I rattle off these stats not only because I like the way they sound—they're music to my ears—but also because any athlete worth his or her weight in salt is comforted by past accomplishments. Athletic accomplishments are often elusive and almost always hard-earned. We want to remember them with exclamation points!!

I also remember that sometime during spring training we played the Yankees. I gave up only two hits that day, but one of them was a line drive over shortstop by Joe D. After the game I was on the train going to the next city when umpire Larry Goetz approached me.

"Hey, Ralph," he said. "I got a compliment for you."

"Who from?"

"Joe D."

"You got to be kidding. He hit my fastball on the screws."

"Maybe so, but Joe D said you've got the best stuff he's seen all spring."

Coming from Joe D, those words meant the world to me. I just knew that 1947 was going to be my year.

But 1947 would not be remembered as Ralph Branca's year— and justifiably so. There was a far bigger story. In 1947 Jackie Robinson made a huge mark on America baseball—as well as history, culture, and society; it was the year he became the first black big leaguer. I was merely lucky enough to be around when that happened. I was a witness to history. And I was also deeply fortunate to be able to befriend a man of extraordinary ability, intelligence, and guts. I loved Jackie and was privileged to call him a teammate and friend.

Scouted by Clyde Sukeforth in California and the Negro Leagues, Robinson had been handpicked by Branch Rickey to integrate the game. The process would unfold during the winter and into the spring of '47.

Jackie's arrival coincided with other major events, if not in the chronicle of the world, then surely in the chronicle of sports. Gil Hodges returned from service. And a rookie outfielder from Los Angeles, Edwin Snider, nicknamed Duke, also joined the team. Along with Pee Wee and Jackie, these 1947 Dodgers would eventually take their place in the pantheon of Brooklyn gods. Before that, though, the history had to be written.

I had read about Jackie, of course. There was that article from '46 when he was brought to Montreal. And there were always rumors that Rickey was bringing him to Brooklyn. Management, though, didn't discuss any of this with the players. And we didn't ask. Because of the large number of Southerners on the team, we all knew the potential for conflict, so we simply avoided the subject.

I knew that Robinson had gone to UCLA, where he excelled at football, baseball, basketball, and track. I also knew he had gone to Officer Candidate School during the war, where his strong sense of racial pride had challenged his military superiors. He had been court-marshaled—and acquitted—for insubordination, the result of his railing against anti-Negro remarks made when he refused to move to the back of an army bus. All that fascinated me, but I wanted to know whether the legend of his athletic accomplishments was overblown. I asked Snider, who had known Jackie from California. They both grew up around L.A.

"Are you kidding?" said Snider. "I remember seeing him when he played football for the Pasadena Junior College Bulldogs. In one game against Compton, my hometown, he ran an incredible kickoff return. He reversed field three or four times. No one could bring him down. He was too quick. Later I went to the campus of UCLA to watch him play baseball. He took all his football running skills and applied them to base running. He was unstoppable. His specialty was stealing home. In the middle of one baseball game, after he put UCLA ahead with two or three hits, he ran over to a track meet already in progress. There was no time to change, so in full uniform he entered the broad jump and wiped out the competition. He jumped 25 feet, just a little less than Jesse Owens's record from 1935. When Jesse Owens went pro, everyone was calling Jackie's older brother Mack the best amateur runner in the country. In 100- and 220-yard dashes, Mack could fly. But I saw Jackie beat his brother. When Jackie put his mind to it, he could beat anyone. Without doubt, he's the most determined competitor I've ever seen. I wouldn't want to play against him. Thank God I get to play *with* him."

Not all the Dodgers felt that way. Pee Wee came from Kentucky. Eddie Stanky, Bobby Bragan, and Dixie Walker lived in

Alabama. Kirby Higbe was from South Carolina. Hugh Casey grew up in Georgia. Pee Wee never expressed racial animus, but Bragan wasn't shy about using the "n" word. Furillo, a Pennsylvanian, was against integration.

Other Dodgers—Durocher, Dressen, Snider, Hodges, Hermanski, and myself—welcomed Jackie. As the team rep, I wasn't shy about arguing with the guys who opposed him. I knew that a couple of them had worked with black guys in gas stations down South.

"What's the difference between that and having a black man on your team?" I asked.

"At the gas station," they said, "they were pumping gas and we were fixing cars. We weren't equal."

"Well, you won't be equal on the ball field either," I shot back. "Jackie's better than you."

My arguments got nowhere.

Before we heard official word that Jackie would be joining us, we went to Havana for spring training. The reason was obvious. We were going to be training with the Montreal Royals, a team that included four blacks—Jackie, up-and-coming catcher Roy Campanella, and pitchers Roy Partlow and big Don Newcombe. Rickey, the mastermind behind the move to sign Jackie, wanted to avoid Florida's racist restrictions.

In Havana, we stayed at the Nacional, a super-swanky hotel overlooking the sea. The Royals stayed in new dorms at a military academy while Jackie, Campy, Don, and Partlow were stuck in a fleabag hotel on the bad side of town.

Playing a few practice games with Montreal, I saw that Jackie was exceptional—but so were Campy and Newk. In my heart, I wished all three could join the Dodgers in the coming season.

No announcement had come down from Rickey. Rumors were flying. Several reporters were saying that Jackie, a shortstop or second baseman, would never make the team because Reese and Stanky commanded both those positions. What the writers didn't know, though, was that, given Robinson's extraordinary adaptability, Rickey planned to put him at first.

That spring training also took us to Caracas, Venezuela, and Panama. It was in Panama where the rumors reached a crescendo. When Rickey refused to deny the fact that he was buying Jackie's contract from Montreal and putting him on the Dodgers, the Southerners decided to take action. They wrote up a petition, arguing that Jackie's presence on the team would be disruptive. Dixie Walker, Hugh Casey, Kirby Higbe, and Bobby Bragan, with support from Furillo, were quick to sign it. Pee Wee refused, and so did most of the others.

Durocher came to Jackie's defense. In no uncertain terms, he let the petitioners have it, screaming, "I don't give a shit if his skin is blue and his ass is green, he's a great player. If we decide to sign him, and you don't like it, you can get the hell off the team. Like it or lump it."

The petition faded away, but the petitioners' attitude did not. They weren't about to sacrifice their salaries, but they sure as hell weren't going to open their hearts or even offer a black man a handshake. Every chance they could, they gave Jackie the cold shoulder.

Jackie rose above the fray. The more disrespect he suffered, the harder he played. Rickey had told him that he wanted a black man tough enough to take the ridicule and keep his dignity. Jackie was more than up to that task. He took ridicule—and then some. I couldn't have done it. If anyone had assaulted me—with ugly curses and vicious taunts—the way Jackie was assaulted, I would have fought back with my fists. But Jackie had a greater vision. He wasn't weak or afraid—he was the strongest proponent for equal rights out there—he was just plain smart. He realized that as a representative of his people, his obligation was to walk through this trial with his head high. A man of strong moral fiber, he'd win more converts by maintaining his cool, not losing it. Like Martin Luther King Jr. after him, he was a leader with a mission. He would allow nothing, not even his explosive temper, to compromise that mission.

On April 10, we were back in Ebbets Field playing the Royals in a series of exhibition games. This was when I faced Jackie for the first time in a big league ballpark. My intention was to pitch him tight and down, but I missed my mark and threw it over the plate, knee-high. Jackie connected, but his sharp grounder went right to Reese. Easy throw to first to end the inning.

On my way back to the dugout, we were crossing paths when Jackie said, "Thanks, Ralph."

I thought about that comment. I thought about Jackie a lot. His presence changed the dynamic of spring training. I'd made a point to seek him out and say, "I've heard great things about you from Snider. I just want you to know that you have my best wishes." Maybe his thank-you was his answer to my cordiality. Or maybe it was his way of saying, "Thanks for throwing it right over the plate." Or maybe he was acknowledging the fact that I refused to sign the stupid petition. Whatever it was, from that day forward Jackie and I became close.

The day before I pitched to him, rumors about Jackie becoming a Dodger were finally relegated to the back of the sports pages. The bigger news was about Leo. All the papers were reporting that Durocher had been banned for a year. The front office hadn't said a word to us. We were shocked.

Here's what happened: Harold Parrott, a former sportswriter who served as the Dodgers' traveling secretary, had ghostwritten an article by Durocher for the *Brooklyn Eagle*. Leo had taken the

72

opportunity to attack Larry MacPhail, general manager of the Yankees.

Enter Dick Young of the *New York Daily News*, eager to spice up the stew. He had heard Rickey say that he'd seen MacPhail seated with two underworld figures at a ball game. If Durocher, who on several occasions had been accused of consorting with gamblers, had been spotted with those guys, all hell would have broken loose. Why the double standard?

When Young went to Leo for a quote, he got what he wanted. Durocher went off: "Where does MacPhail come off flaunting his company with known gamblers right in the players' faces?" asked Durocher. "If I even say 'hello' to one of these guys, I'd be called up before Commissioner Chandler and probably barred."

The result of Leo's published quote was that Commissioner Happy Chandler barred him from baseball for a year.

To us, Durocher's banishment seemed overly harsh. But there was more to it than simply his attack on MacPhail. Leo had married movie star Laraine Day, a wonderful lady who was recently divorced. The extremely strict Catholic Youth Organization didn't like the notoriety surrounding Durocher. They'd been threatening to boycott baseball if he wasn't censored. The Brooklyn branch of the CYO pulled all their boys out of the Dodgers' Knothole Gang, a fraternity of young fans who supported our team.

No doubt, Leo got the shaft. Rickey, though, was intent on keeping the news positive. So on April 10, in the sixth inning of that same game I was pitching against Jackie—in fact, at that exact moment I got him to bunt into a double play—Dodger management issued an official press release announcing that Rickey was buying Robinson's contract from the Royals, thus hiring the first African-American to play in the majors in the modern era. He was given the minimum salary of $5,000.

When Jackie showed up at our clubhouse to put on his uniform, with his soon-to-be famous number 42, I made a point to shake his hand. Gene Hermanski did the same. I know that Duke and Gil treated him with respect, and Pee Wee did not avoid him, yet the atmosphere remained cold and tense. His teammates hardly threw him a welcoming party. Remembering that first encounter years later, Jackie said, "I still felt like a stranger or an uninvited guest." Nonetheless, he was there, and our season was about to start. We were about to jump into the pennant fight, not knowing what to expect. We did know, though, that the lily-white game of baseball was a thing of the past—and this bold move on the part of the Dodgers was the reason why.

On April 15, Opening Day, more rumors. People were saying that an assassin had his sights set on Jackie. In spite of—or maybe because of—that rumor, I stood next to him when we lined up on the field for introductions. Hell, I was proud to stand next to him. At 28, Jack Roosevelt Robinson had already proven himself a champion in many ways. The fact that he was now my teammate and friend brought me comfort.

After the game, in which we beat the Cards 5–3 with Jackie scoring the winning run, my brother said, "Ralphie, you were crazy to stand next to him. What if some sharpshooter missed him by three feet and got you instead?"

"I'd die a hero," I said. "There are worse ways to go."

For me, the season got off to a dismal start. In my first appearance, the Giants whipped me 4–3 in the Polo Grounds. For the rest of the year, I'd wind up pitching every four days and relieving seven times. These days pitchers work every five days. If you ask me— and no one has—I think four days is better. Your arm tends to get less sore when, with proper training and a judicious number of warm-ups, you pitch with 72 hours rest rather than 96. Pitchers have to be cautious, but they don't have to be pampered.

Toward the end of April I felt encouraged after shutting out the Phils 2–0. Philadelphia was murder on Jackie. The Phils showed no mercy. In his memoirs, Jackie remembered them screaming at him, "Hey, black nigger—why don't you go back where you came from?" And that was among the milder comments. Ben Chapman, the Phils manager, would scream, "Hey, boy, I need a shine. Come over here and shine my shoes." Or, "Hey, boy, how come you ain't pickin' cotton? Let me rub your nappy head." Or, "Shouldn't you be working as a porter on some train?"

Throughout the year, watermelons were thrown on the field, not to mention cotton balls and black cats. In St. Louis, the Chase Hotel had black entertainers such as Cab Calloway, Lena Horne, and Billy Eckstine starring in their nightclubs, yet blacks were not permitted to stay there. Jackie was relegated to a third-class hotel across town.

As the weeks went by, discomfort and fury were written all over Jackie's face. I knew he wanted to lash out, but he never dishonored his agreement with Rickey to maintain dignity. For his first three years in the majors, he kept his cool. He showed those racist bastards more respect than they ever showed him.

Our first trip to Cincy had us wondering. After all, the city was right across the river from Kentucky, Pee Wee's home and a state not known for racial tolerance. By then Pee Wee had more than adjusted to Jackie's presence. He'd become Jackie's booster. After seeing Jackie in action, Pee Wee told me, "I'm just glad he doesn't want to play shortstop or I'd be out on my ass." Before the game, as the fans started getting on Jackie, Pee Wee made a point of going from his position at shortstop over to his teammate at first base and putting his arm around him, while staring down the Cincinnati dugout. That gesture said it all.

As Jackie, accompanied by black reporters, traveled from city to city, not only did he face cruel and coarse taunting, but he was also under pressure to appear before many audiences of African Americans who wanted to hear this college-educated gentleman speak. All this happened in the midst of a demanding baseball season. Even as he was in great demand as a leader, he was the object of vicious abuse.

I missed Durocher and disliked his replacement, Burt Shotton. When the commissioner booted Leo for the year, Rickey tried to get ex-Yankee manager, Joe McCarthy, but Joe said no. Coach Clyde Sukeforth managed our first two games, but wasn't interested in the big job. That's when Rickey turned to his old friend Shotton who, at 62, had retired to Florida. He had once managed the Phils and the Reds and coached the Cardinals, the Indians, and the Reds. He had suffered a minor stroke, which is why he wore street clothes. It was hard for him to get into and out of a baseball uniform.

Shotton was a mild-mannered man who, for my money, couldn't hold a candle to Durocher, a baseball wiz. Burt was certainly a gentleman, but he lacked the fire that players need in a manager. Every day he sat in the dugout and kept a perfectly rendered box score. I thought, *What in hell is a manager doing with a box score? Shouldn't he be strategizing instead of making scratches with his perpetually sharpened pencil?* As a baseball mind, Shotton was mediocre, I thought. Rickey liked him, though, because Rickey controlled him.

When we had a day off in New York, I stayed at home with the family. That was always a treat. I wasn't big on nightclubs or parties. But I did love the singing of a guy we called Francis Albert Sinatra. All Italo Americans were and still are crazy for Sinatra. Anyone with the slightest semblance of a musical ear is crazy for Sinatra.

In the forties, Sinatra was knocking 'em dead at the Paramount. An aspiring singer myself, I'd been following his career since he sat on the bandstand first with Harry James and Tommy Dorsey. "All or Nothing at All," his first hit, was all I had to hear. I knew he was the best.

My forever friend from Mount Vernon, Frank Casucci, got tickets to see Sinatra at the Paramount. In those days, the singer came on before the movie. I can't remember the movie—it might have been *Gentlemen's Agreement*—but I sure remember Sinatra. He was sensational.

"Let's go back and see him," said Frank after the show. Frank was a lot gutsier than me.

"We'll never get in," I said.

"We will when I tell him who I'm with," Frank explained. "He's a baseball fan."

We found our way backstage. I was sure some security guy would throw us out, but there we were, standing in front of Sinatra's dressing room. The only thing between us and the man was a bodyguard blocking the door.

"Tell Mr. S that Ralph Branca is here to give his regards," said Casucci. "Ralph Branca of the Brooklyn Dodgers."

Five minutes later, much to my amazement, we were ushered in.

Sinatra, skinny as a beanpole, was sitting on a stool wearing tux pants and an undershirt. His blue eyes lit up when he saw me.

"Big Ralph," he said, extending his hand. "How could they do that to Durocher?"

"It wasn't fair, Frank," I said. "It wasn't right."

"Do you think he'll win on appeal? It's a crime to keep him out the whole season."

"I want him back as badly as you do, Frank."

"And this colored boy, what do you think of him?"

"I like him. Jackie's great."

"I like him, too, Ralph. I like him enough to predict that he'll bring you the big prize this year."

"From your mouth to God's ear, Frank."

"Well, good luck to you, kid."

"Thanks for the great music."

"Just keep that arm limber. And if you see Leo before I do, give him a big wet kiss on the cheek."

"I don't think Leo would like that, Frank."

"If you tell him it's from me, he'll love it." Sinatra laughed and sent me on my way.

The encounter with Sinatra might have helped. From mid-June through mid-July I won seven straight. At the All-Star break I was 14–7.

Despite the fact that we were having a helluva season, Shotton's strategy—or lack thereof—continued to bother me. He was a tired old man who did nothing to energize the team. Fortunately, we had enough energy of our own. Our pitching was strong and Jackie, under unbelievable pressure, was having a sensational rookie year—not to mention solid hitting by Dixie, Reiser, Furillo, and catcher Bruce Edwards.

On July 18, I won my 15th game, a one-hitter against the Cards. That night game at Ebbets Field is remembered, however, not for what I did but because of what happened to Jackie—a vicious assault that could have ended his career.

I retired the first 12 batters I faced when Enos "Country" Slaughter came up in the top of the fifth. Slaughter was tough, an excellent hitter who ran the bases hard. A North Carolinian, he didn't hide his disdain for blacks. He didn't like how Jackie had integrated the game.

Enos grounded to the right side of the infield. As is standard, I automatically broke left to cover first base in case Jackie fielded the ball. But it was Stanky's play at second. Eddie scooped it up for an easy toss to Jackie. I was 15 feet away and had a perfect view of what happened next:

As Jackie stretched to make the catch, Slaughter deliberately went after him and viciously stepped on his calf with his spikes. Jackie didn't drop the ball—Slaughter was out—but I could see him writhing in pain. Our trainer, Doc Wendler, ran out to take a look. It was a deep, bloody gash, yet Jackie wouldn't leave the game. He knew he was lucky. Later Doc told us that Jackie could have been maimed.

"Next time the son of a bitch comes up," I told Jackie, "I'll get him for you."

"No, Ralph," he said. "Just keep pitching like you're pitching."

When Slaughter came up at the top of the eighth, I had retired 21 in a row and was pitching a perfect game. I thought about sticking it in Enos's ribs, but instead took Jackie's advice. Slaughter got lucky and hit a seeing-eye grounder between Stanky and Jackie for the first and only Cardinal hit of the game. After Enos's fluke single, I gave up a walk, but then retired the next six batters to win the game 7–0. It was a one-hit, one-walk near-perfect game, but I still regret that I didn't knock Enos on his ass for going after Jackie.

As July turned into August, we were nine games ahead of the second-place Giants. In the American League, the Yankees were leading the Red Sox and Tigers by a dozen games. A subway series was in the making.

We rolled into Chicago, where I was set to pitch the final game of a weekend series. The Cubs won 10–8 on Friday and on Saturday walloped us 12–2. During the Saturday game, the first two hitters in their lineup—Peanuts Lowrey and Eddie Waitkus—each went five for six and between them drove in eight runs. On Sunday, after walking pitcher Johnny Schmitz—a no-no—in the third, I faced Lowrey, certain he'd bunt. Instead he whacked a line drive to right field, barely missing Jackie's ear. Jackie had also anticipated a bunt and had charged in from first base.

In the fifth inning I knew Lowrey was leading off. On the way out of the dugout, I told my catcher, Bruce Edwards, "Lowrey's wearing us out. I'm knocking him down on the first pitch."

When the first pitch went sailing over his head, a foot too high, I silently cursed myself. *What the hell's wrong with you, Branca? You can't even throw a good knockdown?*

My roommate Eddie Stanky, at second base, saw me mumbling to myself and came over. "What's wrong, big boy?" he asked. "What's eating you?"

"I gotta get this guy," I said, referring to Lowrey. "I'm really going to show him a good knockdown!"

"That's what I wanna hear," said Stanky. "Go get him!"

My next throw was a picture-perfect knockdown pitch at his shoulder. His hat went flying, his bat went sailing, and Lowrey was on the ground. Two pitches later, though, I wound up walking him.

Next up was Waitkus, the other Cub who was wearing us out. I decided to give him something to worry about. I only wanted to knock him down, but I stuck it in his ribs. This got Shotton upset. Shotton, who never came to the mound (he couldn't because he was not in uniform), sent coach Clyde Sukeforth.

"What's the matter with you, kid?" asked Clyde. "Aren't you trying to win?"

"I'm protecting my hitters," I said. "That's what I'm trying to do."

Frustrated, I threw the ball down. It hit the rubber and bounced 20 feet into the air. Shotton gave me the hook.

After the game he gave me a piece of his mind. He called me to his office and said, "I heard you tell Edwards you were going to knock Lowrey down on your first pitch. So you were throwing at him intentionally."

"Sure."

Shotton knew damn well that there are times when pitchers need to throw hitters off balance, especially the hitters who are red hot. That was one of those times.

"You could have killed him."

"My purpose was to scare, not to maim."

"If you killed him, that would have been premeditated murder," said Shotton.

"Never in a million years would I have killed him."

"But if you had," said my manager, "being of your ilk, you wouldn't have thought anything of it."

"*My ilk?* What the hell does that mean?"

"You can figure it out yourself, Branca, but the meaning is clear."

I started to say something, but remembered that I was in the last months of a season where I was 16–5. I was determined to win 20 and I didn't want anything to get in my way. Rather than get fined and lose playing time, I kept quiet.

I got fined anyway. A hundred fifty bucks. When Dixie Walker heard about it, he called a team meeting and said, "This kid Branca is pitching his ass off for us. He's doing a helluva job. If he wants to brush back a hitter now and then, well, that's how the game is supposed to be played. This fine is ridiculous. So let's help out Ralphie and throw a couple of bucks in the kitty and pay this fine for him."

Jackie was the first to contribute, and the others followed.

When we got to St. Louis on September 11 for a critical series, the pennant race had tightened up. We were only four and a half games ahead of the Cards. I won my 20th that day but, again, Jackie had a scare. This time it was Joe Garagiola who stepped on Jackie's foot at first. I didn't see it as intentional—it wasn't anything like Slaughter's vicious assault—but when Jackie came up to bat, he said something to Joe. Joe said something back, and, just like that, Joe threw off his mask and was nose-to-nose with Jackie. Knowing Joe, I was certain he had no racial motives. At this point, though, after months of taking abuse, Jackie's nerves were frail. Fortunately, he and Joe didn't come to blows. The next blow Jackie struck was a two-run home run, and we won the game 4–3.

We lost on Friday, but fought back on Saturday to take an 8–7 thriller. In that game, Jackie went two for four and scored twice, but experienced another perilous moment. I was in the dugout and Jackie ran over in foul territory, directly in front of me, to make a catch. He was going full force and didn't realize that the warm-up mound was in his path. As he hit the mound, he was able to catch the ball but tripped and was about to crash into the dugout. I jumped out of the dugout and made a perfect right shoulder tackle on him. I caught him and kept him from falling. He wound up in my arms. In describing the scene, someone said that Jackie and I looked like a married couple.

After the game, in which Jackie went two for four and scored twice, ensuring our one-run victory, we were in the locker room, chatting.

"Hey," I said, "I bet there aren't many guys who can say they made a clean tackle on Jackie Robinson."

"Few in football," said Jackie, "and you're the first in baseball."

As we undressed, he started complaining about the strawberry, a nasty skin abrasion, on his thigh.

"I wouldn't call that a strawberry," I said. "For you, I'd call it a blackberry."

"You're the only guy who could get away with saying something like that," said Jackie. "Anyone else I'd have to run over."

"Only to be tackled. I did it once, Jackie, and I'll do it again."

After the game, we had a quick dinner, a few laughs, and a discussion about the need to press even harder in the final weeks of the pennant race.

We held our ground. With Jackie setting a torrid pace, we finished the season five games ahead of the Cards and were ready to tackle the Yankees in the World Series. For my money, there's nothing more exciting in sports than a subway Series—and this was going to be a doozy.

September 30, 1947. Some 73,000 fans were in their seats and hanging from the rafters at Yankee Stadium.

"As the premier thrower on the Dodgers," one writer predicted, "Branca is sure to get the nod for game one."

I did.

Butterflies?

A few, but believe me, I was feeling more determination than fear. More eagerness than anxiety. *Let me get out there and show my hometown what I got.*

My family—Mom, Dad, all my brothers and sisters—were in the stands. A beautiful day for the Branca clan.

No doubt the Yankees were formidable. Hell, the Yankees were always formidable. Starting in late June, they won 19 in a row, knocking all contenders out of the race. Their big pitchers were Allie Reynolds (19–8), Spec Shea (14–5), and Joe Page (14–8). Their big star was Joe D, who hit .315 with 20 home runs. In terms of press coverage, though, the biggest star of the Series was Jackie. In every way, this was Jackie's year.

He could have buckled under the pressure. He could have ripped off the heads of hundreds of hecklers. He could have cursed back, fought back, lost his temper—and all with absolute justification. But not only had he maintained his decorum, he also had played magnificently: during the 1947 season he had hit .297 and led the major leagues with 29 stolen bases to become the first winner of the newly established Rookie of the Year Award. Beyond the stats, he brought a new brash style to the big leagues. It was, to be sure, a smart and daring style cultivated in the Negro Leagues, where daredevil running and hitting, executed with dramatic flair, delighted the fans.

If the World Series of '47 set records for attendance and national interest, Robinson was the reason. Whether rooting for or against him, everyone wanted to see this man in action.

In that first game, I felt terrific going to the mound. After all, at 21, I was the youngest pitcher ever to start the first game of a World Series. This was also the first World Series ever to be broadcast via a new invention called television.

On that Tuesday afternoon in the Bronx, my ball had good movement. I mowed down the first 12 men I faced. But I stumbled in the fifth. Joe D beat a grounder to deep short. I walked first baseman George McQuinn and hit third baseman Billy Johnson. Bases loaded, no outs. I was in a jam.

Sukeforth didn't come to the mound to give advice or settle me down. I tried to settle myself down. I didn't mind pressure situations. I stared in for the sign and then delivered a fastball to Johnny Lindell at the knees. He drilled it to left for a double, scoring Joe D and McQuinn. Johnson was at third, Lindell at second. Still no word from my manager or coach.

With first base open, I pitched carefully to Phil Rizzuto, who drew a walk. With the bases loaded, Sukeforth finally ran from the dugout.

"Go take a shower, kid," he said.

I wanted to say, *Where were you when I was in trouble? Shouldn't you have been out here to give me a break and a pause to catch my breath?* But I didn't say a word.

The Yanks wound up winning 5–3.

In game two, with Allie Reynolds on the mound, the Yanks won again, 10–3.

The Yankees led the Series, two games to zip.

From Yankee Stadium we moved to Ebbets for the next three games.

Game Three was critical. We had to win or we were toast. Hilda had her cowbell. The Dodger Sym-phony was louder than ever. The fans were screaming their heads off. In the second inning, we busted out with six runs and the place went wild. But in the fifth, the score was Bums 9, Yanks 6, when I was called to relieve. I was surprised. My expectation was that I'd start either game four or game five. I was a starter, not a reliever, but of course I was eager to try to hold down the fort. I got us out of the inning, but in the sixth gave up two doubles and a run. Bums 9, Yanks 7. In the top of the eighth, after Rizzuto popped out, a pinch hitter stepped to the plate: Yogi Berra.

Busier keeping his box score than providing us with scouting reports, Shotton had told us nothing about Yogi. My first pitch, a high fastball, was overthrown, and Berra drove it all the way out. For the first time in Series history, a pinch hitter had hit a round-tripper. Now it was Bums 9, Yanks 8, and I was yanked out of the game. We managed to hold on for the win, though, and were back in the Series, down only two games to one.

In the clubhouse after the game, Sukeforth called me over.

"Ralph, didn't you know Berra's a first-pitch fastball hitter who likes 'em high?"

"No, I didn't know." I wanted to tell Sukeforth that he never gave me a scouting report, but I kept my mouth closed. I was looking for my next start.

It never came.

Game four was another thriller. In the bottom of the ninth, the Yankees' Bill Bevens was working on a no-hitter. We were losing 2–1. With men on first and second, we were down to our last out. Lose today and the Yanks would be up three games to one. Pinch hitter Cookie Lavagetto was our last hope.

Cookie delivered! He smashed a double that scored pinch runners Al Gionfriddo and Eddie Miksis: The Dodgers won! The Series was tied!

I figured I'd start game 5. I figured wrong.

Game 5 was another pitchers' duel, but I wasn't in it. Spec Shea threw a gem, allowing only four Dodger hits and one run. They beat us 2–1 and led the Series 3–2. We now needed to win two in a row at the Stadium.

The fever pitch of this subway Series was something to behold. As I rode the train to the game, all the men—and many of the women—held copies of the *News*, *Post*, *Mirror*, *Journal-American*, *World Telegram*, *Herald Tribune*, and *Times* over their faces. The headlines screamed the news—BUMS ON THE ROPES!—and every discussion involved Joe D or Jackie. Walking down the streets of the Bronx, the apartment windows were open, and when Perry Como wasn't singing "Chi-Baba, Chi-Baba (My Bambino Goes to Sleep)" or Vaughn Monroe wasn't crooning "Ballerina," the announcer was getting the borough all worked up about game six.

The game is best remembered for a single act: Al Gionfriddo's magnificent catch of Joe D's towering drive that sailed some 400-plus feet. I've got to give Shotton credit. We were ahead 8–5 in the bottom of the 6th. Snuffy Stirnweiss and Berra were on base. In a defensive move, Shotton put Gionfriddo in left field. It was the perfect substitution because Al had the speed to chase down Joe D's shot, reach over the fence, and make a magnificent catch, thus saving two runs. The camera caught Joe D as he shook his head in disappointment and kicked the dirt at second base. It became a classic moment, and, once again, we tied the Series. Because I relieved for two innings, I got the win, but it was hardly deserved. Al secured us the victory.

Back to the Sinatra song "All or Nothing at All." If we could win game seven, we'd win the first world championship in Dodger history. We could think of nothing else but winning. I could think of nothing else but starting the game.

Shotton started Hal Gregg, who was 4–5 for the year with an ERA of 5.87. By then, it didn't really matter to me. I just wanted us to win. Burton could put his mother on the mound if her changeup fooled the Yankees.

We scored first. In the top of the second, Gene Hermanski's triple and Spider Jorgensen's double led to two runs. Sadly, that was the last time we scored in the game. Our bats went dead while the Yanks managed five runs off five Dodger pitchers. I saw no action.

The season—my best and, because of Jackie, perhaps the most important in baseball history—ended on a down note.

I took the subway home to Mount Vernon.

The Buildup

MOST GREAT TEAMS take time to gel. The Brooklyn Dodgers were no different. Reiser and Reese were among the first building blocks. Pee Wee would continue to be a fixture at short while Reiser would be traded to the Braves after the 1948 season. In 1948, joining a lineup that already included dangerous hitters such as Jackie, Furillo, and Hermanski, two future stars arrived: Roy Campanella and Billy Cox. Our pitching staff also was bolstered by two great hurlers: Carl Erskine from Anderson, Indiana, and the guileless Preacher Roe from Viola, Arkansas. Cox and Roe were traded from the Pirates. Campy and Oisk were called up from the minors.

Defensively, beautiful things were about to happen. Edwards and Hodges no longer needed to catch, since Campy would command that position with remarkable results for years to come. Gil moved over to first base, allowing Jackie to play second, where he felt most comfortable. (My friend Eddie Stanky, longtime Dodger second baseman, was traded to the Braves.) At third, Billy Cox would prove to be one of the premier fielders of his generation. You have to think ahead to guys like Mike Schmidt or Brooks Robinson to categorize Billy's superior skill at playing the hot corner.

Jackie's arrival in '47 had energized every aspect of the game for players and fans alike. Jackie brought the fire. Hodges brought

89

his own kind of savvy. He was a devout student of the game, a power hitter and future Gold Glove fielder whose even temperament and wry wit would endear him to everyone. At 6'1" and 210 pounds, Gil was all muscle. His Mr. Universe physique was the best in the big leagues. His strength made us all stronger.

The contrast between Jackie and Campy was pronounced. Jackie was an assertive spirit when it came to politics and race; Campy had far less interest in such matters. Sometimes the two clashed. The contrast between Jackie and Campy was fascinating— hot-tempered Robinson and mild-mannered Roy. There were moments when Jackie considered Campy too passive, and times when Campy deemed Jackie too militant. There also was an undercurrent of competition between the two. I think Campy may have wanted to share more of the spotlight with Jackie. Of course, Campy would earn his own chunk of immortality. As a three-time MVP, he was the backbone of the iconic Dodger teams of the fifties.

Candidly, Campy was not my favorite catcher, not because he wasn't great, but because he never gave me a low target. As a fastball pitcher, I liked a knee-high target, the kind that Bruce Edwards, Gil Hodges, and later Rube Walker gave me. The low target favored curveball pitchers such as Carl, who liked to see that big mitt below the knees.

Erskine was a bright man—he'd wind up as a bank president and financial wiz. Carl had one of the sneakiest fastballs in the game, a great curve, excellent changeup, and tremendous poise on the mound. In the late forties, he was a starter and a reliever. In the fifties, he made the rotation, won 20 in '53, and struck out 14 in the World Series.

Oisk was my age when he joined the team—21—whereas Preacher Roe was 31. Roe had been around. He picked up the name Preacher because, if no one were in the room, he wouldn't mind talking to the wall. Elwin Charles Roe had pinpoint control. His overhand curve was excellent. What he called his slider was really a spitter; he'd wet his fingers with saliva before grasping the ball. Preacher was a slippery character and a good guy.

We went to spring training in the winter of '48 in the Dominican Republic. Despite the Series loss five months earlier, our spirits were high. Leo showed up with his lovely wife, Laraine Day, and was eager to whip us into shape. His year of banishment made him want to win that much more. Nothing was going to get in his way. Seeing Jackie for the first time, Leo went after him, exclaiming, "Oh, shit, Robinson, you look like the fat lady at the circus. You aren't pregnant with twins, are you?"

Jackie had come to camp 25 pounds overweight.

Leo kept him on. "We're going to have to roll you around the bases," he prodded. "Your legs will collapse under all that goddamn weight."

In his memoirs, Jackie admitted that Leo, whom he called a "magnificent tongue-lasher," was right, but didn't like how Durocher voiced these insults in front of the press. Ultimately, Jackie worked off the weight, but the cost was a slow start to his second season.

I also had a slow start.

Before Opening Day, Branch Rickey called me into his office. He was on his throne, sucking his unlit cigar, and eager to pontificate.

"Branca," he said, "last year you walked too many and didn't complete enough games."

I was bewildered.

"I led the staff last year," I said. "I won 21 games."

"You don't want to rest on your laurels, do you?"

"No. This year I want to win 25."

"Well, that's precisely my point. To do that, you'll have to find a way to cut down on your bases on balls. I suggest you work on your control."

"I'm trying," I said.

"And I'm telling you that it's imperative for you to try harder."

I left Rickey's office in a daze. He hadn't given me a single compliment. All he did was make me anxious. I also wondered why Rickey—and not Durocher—was talking to me like this. If anyone was to upbraid me, shouldn't it be my manager? Was it the business of the club president to single out players for criticism? Either way, I was rattled. He put pressure on me that I did not need. I averaged three walks and five-plus strikeouts a game. Nothing wrong with that. Later I figured it out. Rickey knew I had great potential and would be a premier pitcher for years to come, barring injuries, and I would be worthy of being paid a big salary. In other words, a Rickey no-no. Instead of applauding me for a great season in 1947, he denigrated my accomplishments to sign me for less than I was worth. I made $6,500 in 1947 and asked for $15,000 in '48, but he got me to accept $12,500. Larry Jansen of the New York Giants also won 21 in 1947, while signing for $6,000. In the middle of the year Horace Stoneham, the Giant owner and general manager, tore up his contract and raised it to $10,000, and in 1948 he made $17,000—a little different from the $19,000 I made in those two years. Thank you, Mr. Rickey!

P.S.: We won the pennant in 1947.

On May 6, I was 1–3 and struggling. Rickey's words of discouragement were on my mind; I didn't want to walk anyone. I was trying to complete the first game of a doubleheader in Pittsburgh. Overthrowing, though, I had walked a couple of runners. Pee Wee was nursing an injury, so Gene Mauch had replaced him at shortstop. Gene came running to the mound.

"You look jittery, Ralphie," he said.

I hesitated, looking over at the dugout to see if Leo was going to yank me.

"Is he coming to take me out?" I asked.

"What are you talking about?" asked Gene. "You're the best pitcher in the league. Now prove it."

Leo, who kept pacing back and forth, didn't yank me. He wanted to see what I would do with Ralph Kiner. By the end of the season, Kiner would hit 40 homers. (He had hit 51 in '47 and would hit 54 in '49.) He had clobbered a homer off me in Ebbets Field. Before this game in Pittsburgh, he had watched me warming up and said, "Stud"—Kiner called everyone "stud"—"you better have your best stuff today."

I had watched my teammate Erv Palica try to get his curveball over on Kiner, only to get tagged for a four-bagger. I knew not to throw a curve, and Mauch's pep talk had restored my confidence. It's amazing how an encouraging word can boost a pitcher's morale.

I was able to overpower Kiner with speed and, in doing so, completed and won that game.

Between May 27 and June 25, I won seven in a row.

By the All-Star break I was 10–6 with an ERA of 3.29. I was on track to win 20. There was even a Ralph Branca Appreciation Day, which began in Mount Vernon. Busloads of my fellow towns-folk, including the mayor and two priests from our church, took the long ride to Ebbets Field, where they showered me with love. Naturally, I loved them back.

However, the Dodger team as a whole was underperforming. In midsummer we found ourselves in the middle of the pack, eight and a half games behind the Braves.

I started the All-Star game on July 13 in St. Louis, where I gave up two runs in three innings. As I pitched that game, though, I knew something was very wrong, the result of an injury I had suffered at St. Louis a couple of weeks earlier.

On June 26, before a game with the Cardinals, Billy Cox and Tommy Brown, my least favorite Dodger, were warming up. I was nearby playing pepper. Brown used the occasion to show off his arm and, instead of throwing normally, shot a wild bullet that missed Cox's glove and caught me on the shin. I went down, and the next thing I knew I was in the dugout. Doc Wendler told me to pull down my sock. It looked terrible—the bruise was huge—and I asked Doc whether I should skip my pregame running routine.

"No reason to," he said. "This isn't anything. You can run."

So I did my running.

Doc was dead wrong. I'd pitched the night before and won 1–0. This was 14 hours later. It was 104 degrees on the field. A well-trained doctor would have given me different instructions.

I pitched three more games before the All-Star break, but increasingly knew something was not right. After the break, I pitched in Boston and on the train to Philly saw that my leg had swollen dramatically. The lining of the bone, now infected, had to be drained. The doctors told me that I should never have run after the initial injury. My shin had required ice and rest, not exertion.

Our trainer's mistake cost me dearly. I developed periosteomyelitis and was hospitalized for more than two weeks, and remained on the disabled list for five. I was never the same again. The infection went to my arm. I won only two games the last half of the year. My ineffectiveness limited our pennant chances for seasons to come.

But the most shocking news to come after the All-Star break involved Durocher. Branch never liked Leo, and when the Dodgers faltered in '48, Rickey made Leo the scapegoat. In turn, Leo lashed back at Rickey through the press. The bad blood between the two men had turned toxic.

Giants owner Horace Stoneham called Rickey to tell him that he was firing Manager Mel Ott, my childhood hero. Stoneham wanted permission to speak with Burt Shotton. Permission denied. Rickey told Stoneham that he might need Shotton, but by all means talk to Durocher. Stoneham was shocked. Leo was the very essence of the Dodgers. Fans could see losing the Brooklyn Bridge to the Bronx before losing Leo. Rickey had to be kidding.

He wasn't. He'd fire Durocher so Horace could hire him. It happened in a flash. And just like that, in the middle of the 1948 season, Leo was managing the Giants and old Burt Shotton, with his sturdy box score, was back in the Brooklyn manager's slot.

Never comfortable with Leo, Jackie was happy. I was not. I knew Durocher was a super-shrewd manager. Moreover, he saw in me a lot of the same gutsy determination that he displayed. That's why I wasn't surprised when one of his first moves was to ask Rickey to trade me for Bobby Thomson. Would I have gone? How would I have felt about leaving Brooklyn, sticking with Leo, and playing for a team that I loved as a kid? Those are hard questions. By then I was a devoted Dodger. The team had brotherhood and soul. It wouldn't have been easy. On the other hand, given the reserve clause, I'd have no choice. Rickey nixed the trade.

On August 16, after winning in Boston, we trailed the first-place Braves by only two games. The next day, on the train to Philly, someone handed me a newspaper. My heart sank when I read the headline: BABE RUTH DEAD AT 53. If anyone was immortal, it was the great Babe. For all my childhood love of the Giants and my adult love for the Dodgers, when anyone asked who is the greatest ballplayer of all time, my answer was, and always will be, the Babe. Think about it . . .

He pitched for ten years and never had a losing record. Overall he was 94–46 with an ERA of 2.28. Ruth pitched 29 2/3 scoreless World Series innings, a record that held for four decades until Whitey Ford reached 33 2/3. As a hitter, Babe's lifetime average was .342, remarkable for a slugger. What's more, he had 2,873 hits and 714 homers; every 11.7 times he came to the plate he connected for a round-tripper. For my money, no one can touch the Bambino.

Back in the late summer of '48 the Dodgers stumbled as the Braves streaked. That was the Boston team of Warren Spahn and

Johnny Sain. We had a saying, "Spahn, Sain, and pray for rain." Their pitching was brilliant, and their hitters—led by Alvin Dark, Jeff Heath, and Tommy Holmes—terrific. They won the pennant easily, only to lose the Series 4–2 to the great Cleveland Indians team of Bob Lemon, Bob Feller, Lou Boudreau, Dale Mitchell, and Larry Doby, the first African American to play in the American League.

I went home to Mount Vernon and watched the winter kick in. I decided to barnstorm around the country with a team of major leaguers, among them Bobby Thomson. He seemed like a good guy. I didn't know whether he'd been told that Leo wanted to trade him for me, and didn't say anything. No need for hard feelings.

After the barnstorming tour I took a detour from baseball. Something else was calling me. You might say it was music to my ears.

"Polka Dots and Moonbeams"

I ADMIT IT; I'M proud of my voice. I'm not saying I'm Sinatra, but I think I'm pretty good. I have a strong baritone/bass and can carry a tune with something that resembles style. I was good enough to be invited to sing "Lucky Old Sun" on *The Ed Sullivan Show*. Jinx Falkenburg and her husband, Tex McCrary, had a radio program, *Hi Jinx*, where I also performed. Jackie Robinson also hosted a radio show and had me on as a mystery guest. Listeners had to guess the vocalist singing a parody of "Slow Boat to China." No one could identify me.

Determined to hone my craft, I found a voice teacher. Then I found an agent. Next thing I knew I was singing at nightclubs in Saratoga Springs, Montreal, New York, and Long Branch, New Jersey. I wasn't exactly playing the Copa, but I was having fun. I had a good rapport with audiences. At first they were intrigued with the novelty of a singing pitcher, but after a few numbers they seemed to forget that I was a jock. During the off-season, show business was a pleasant diversion from baseball. Maybe after I retired from the game, I thought, I'd hit the stage full-time. It was something to consider. For the time being, though, I saw my future with the Dodgers.

•

In my early twenties, I was still tied to my family—my parents, sisters, brothers, grandfather, aunts, and uncles, all of whom were my biggest boosters. When it came to girls, I was hardly assertive. Among college and baseball and singing, I had enough to do without the complications of romance. So when I got a fateful call from a friend, I wasn't especially enthusiastic.

"Ralphie," said Wolfgang Cribari, a highly respected attorney in Westchester County, "how'd you like to double-date with me Saturday night?"

"I don't know. I'm not dating anyone now," I said.

"Why not? There's this swell dinner at the Westchester Country Club. And dancing, too. You like to dance. Just find a date."

"That's the problem."

"Why is that a problem?"

"I don't know anyone to ask."

"I don't believe you. Big league players have women chasing them all over town."

"Not this big league player."

"Well, think of someone. And do it quickly. We'll have a ball."

Dinner and dancing could be fun, but I hardly had a ready inventory of willing women. As I thought it over, though, someone did come to mind.

Four years before, when I met Ann Mulvey, granddaughter of Steve McKeever, the man who built Ebbets Field, I was taken with her sweetness. She was blond, blue-eyed, and absolutely beautiful. Her smile lit up the day. Every year, she and her parents, Jim and Dearie, came to spring training. They also watched most of our home games from their front-row box behind home plate. I had been noticing Ann for some time. I'd heard that she had enrolled at Marymount, a Catholic college in Tarrytown, not far from Mount Vernon. I got the number of the school and called. There was a pay phone in the dorm, and it took a while for her to come on the line.

"Ann," I said, "it's Ralph Branca. Do you remember me?"

"Ralph, how could I not remember you? Is there any 21-game winner for the Dodgers that I wouldn't remember?"

"Well, I just meant I had never called you before and . . ." I was tongue-tied. With her sparkling personality, Ann helped me out.

"Not to worry, Ralph. I'm happy to hear from you and eager to hear why you're calling."

"I'm wondering whether you'd like to go out with me?"

"On a date?"

"Yes, there's a dinner dance at the Westchester Country Club Saturday night."

"That sounds like fun."

"So you're willing?"

"Why wouldn't I be?"

"I wasn't sure how your folks felt about you going out with someone five years older than you."

"Since I'm on my own at college, it's not exactly my folks' decision."

"We'll be double-dating with a friend and his girl. Is that okay?"

"Another baseball player?"

"A lawyer."

"As long as he's a Dodger fan."

"I wouldn't bring him along if he wasn't."

At the end of the forties, the big-band era had begun its slow fade. Nonetheless, that night in Westchester, a big band was situated on the patio where a large terrazzo floor accommodated dozens of couples dancing to dreamy romantic music.

The song was "Polka Dots and Moonbeams." The singer sang about a country dance being held in a garden. Her voice, like Jo Stafford's, conveyed soft intimacy. The music was seductive. The night air was crisp, intoxicating. Ann, exquisite in a royal blue dress, danced gracefully. She looked gorgeous, a little like Katharine Hepburn, only prettier. To hold Ann in my arms was, well . . . heaven. Of course I didn't tell her that.

"You're a good dancer," was all I said.

"You're not so bad yourself."

"Thanks."

"When you sing along with the music, I hear you can carry a tune."

"No one told you that I'm a singer?"

"I don't know anything about you—except that you have an impressive fastball and you go after hitters you don't like."

"An exaggeration."

"I've seen you brush back a few Giants in my day."

"Only those who deserved it."

After a couple more dances, we found a quiet bench on the patio where we could be alone.

"How does it look this year?" asked Ann.

"You sound more interested in baseball than I do."

"It's in the family. In my blood."

"Mine, too. I'd say the year looks good."

"Even with Durocher gone?"

"I wish he was back," I admitted. "He's the brainiest manager out there. He's always thinking three or four innings down the line."

"And Shotton?" asked Ann.

"No comment."

"You're discreet."

"I'm out with one of the owner's daughters."

"Is that how you see me?"

"I see you as a lovely young woman who has honored me with her presence tonight."

"Quite a flowery statement coming from an athlete."

"I've been working up the courage to tell you that all night."

"Ralph Branca," she said, "are you one of those tough-on-the-outside but soft-on-the-inside guys?"

"Maybe. Is that kind of guy appealing to you?"

"Maybe," answered Ann with a smile.

At evening's end, I walked her to her front door, took her hand, and gave her a quick kiss on the cheek, a bold move for those days.

"I had a great time," she said. "Thanks, Ralph."

"When will I see you again?" I asked.

"When's your next start?" she answered.

I had to laugh.

I was smitten, but, as inexperienced as I was in courting, I proceeded judiciously. I thought the next move might be a movie.

"Yes," she said, when I called her a week later. "I love movies. I'll be at my parents' house this weekend. Can you pick me up there?"

"I will if I can find it."

"Can you find Ebbets Field?"

"There's a good chance I can."

"Well, we live five blocks away, at 39 Maple Street."

"An apartment building?"

"No," said Ann, "a private home."

It turned out to be a magnificent three-story home of red brick. Ann's grandmother Elizabeth lived next door in an almost-identical but reversed edifice. Her grandfather Steve McKeever had built two mirror-image homes side by side—one for himself and one for his daughter Dearie.

Of course, I had met Ann's folks before, but in the context of the ball field. Now I was showing up at their front door as a man keenly interested in their daughter. I didn't know how they'd react.

Ann's mother, Dearie, reacted beautifully. She said she was thrilled to see me.

"I've been worried about you, Ralph," she said.

"You have?"

"I know you had a serious infection. I saw how that slowed you down, and I've been concerned."

"Thank you, ma'am."

"Is this soreness gone?"

"I'm feeling fine."

"And what about this new pitcher, the one we signed from the Newark Eagles?" They were a team in the Negro National League.

"Oh, Don Newcombe. He's terrific. I think he's going to be great."

"As great as Jackie and Campy?"

"I think so. He's big and strong with tremendous speed. He's got a four-inch curveball that's fooling everyone."

"Glad to hear it, Ralph. I have a feeling that '49 is going to be even better for you than '47."

"Nice of you to say so, Mrs. Mulvey."

"Please call me Dearie."

It was wonderful to be talking to a woman who was as passionate a baseball fan as my own mother.

"Ann's getting dressed," she said. "Come into the study. Jim wants to say hello."

Jim Mulvey, Ann's dad, was at his desk studying some papers. He was a man with a serious demeanor.

"Have a seat, Ralph," he said. "Can I get you something to drink?"

"No, thank you. I don't want to disturb your work."

"You aren't disturbing. I can use a break. My work can get tedious."

"You're an accountant, aren't you, sir?"

"I used to be," he said. "I was a C.P.A. with Price Waterhouse. And then I met Sam Goldwyn."

"The movie producer?"

"The same. He asked me to work up a few budgets on his films, and when I did he was pleased with my work. Long story short, Ralph, I'm now the president of Sam's company."

"So you make movies, Mr. Mulvey?"

"Well, it's actually Sam who makes the movies. I make the deals with the distributors. I try to make sure that the movies make money."

"Of all the movies you've been involved with, what's your favorite?"

"*Pride of the Yankees.* I actually bought the rights to that film from Sam. I own it personally."

"The one about Lou Gehrig?"

"Right. Gary Cooper plays Lou."

"And Babe Ruth plays himself."

"Then you've seen it."

"Twice."

"Talking about films, Ann says that you're taking her to the movies tonight. What do you plan on seeing?"

"They're showing *On the Town* just down the street at the Loew's. Is that one of Samuel Goldwyn's films?"

"Afraid not. It's a different company—MGM. Frank Sinatra and Gene Kelly. Dearie and I saw it last week. You and Ann will love it."

We did. We sat in the balcony and tapped our toes to "New York, New York," a wonderful town where the Bronx is up and the Battery's down. Afterward we had dessert in a little restaurant on Empire Boulevard. I couldn't remember being any happier.

"Your parents are great," I said, "but I was worried that they wouldn't want you going out with a baseball player."

"If you were a Yankee or Giant, you'd be barred from the house. But as a Dodger, you're already family."

"It feels like that," I said.

•

It looked like 1949 was going to be the Dodgers' year. The arrival of Newcombe energized our staff. He'd led all Dodger pitchers that year with 17 wins. Newk was my man. I loved the guy. Maybe it's because big men, especially big pitchers, have instant camaraderie and like to work out together. Or maybe it was because the 6'4" righthander had a competitive spirit as fierce as mine. I also know that, along with Campy, his presence on the team helped Jackie relax. Robinson boosted his average to .342 and won the National League's Most Valuable Player award. (Ted Williams, the American League's MVP, hit .343.) Newcombe shared Jackie's attitude about racial equality. Newk was impatient—and justifiably so—with any kind of prejudice. Don didn't mince words.

During spring training that year, we were riding from Miami to Vero Beach when se stopped at a diner. Stepping off the bus, we saw a "No Coloreds Allowed" sign on the window. Newk, Campy, and Jackie were disgusted.

"No worries, guys," I said. "Just give me your orders. I'll be honored to wait on you. My treat."

They told me what sandwiches and drinks they wanted. I got their food, got some for myself, and we all ate on the bus together.

Other than the pain of racial prejudice, it was a positive year. Preacher Roe, with an ERA of 2.79, would win 15, I'd win 13, Joe Hatten 12, and Jack Banta 10. Erskine, at 8–1, hadn't even reached his prime. Our sluggers—Campy, Hodges, and Snider—each hit more than 20 home runs; Furillo hit 18 and batted .322.

All season long, we were shoulder-to-shoulder with St. Louis. Stan Musial, who finished second to Jackie in the MVP voting, was his incredibly consistent self: .338 average, 36 home runs, 123 RBIs. It was a helluva pennant race.

I was feeling good. At $15,000, I was earning my highest salary. And I also had my best start. Beginning with my first game in April, I won seven straight. When I went to the All-Star game, played in Ebbets Field, the Dodgers were half a game ahead of the Cards and I was 10–3, and having one of my best seasons yet.

Unfortunately, I would struggle after the break, but at the end of September we were still neck-and-neck with the Cards. By beating the Phils at Shibe Park on October 2, we finally clinched the pennant. In three years, this would be our second subway Series with the Yankees who, in a torrid race, had also nabbed the pennant by only a single game, beating the Red Sox in the last two contests of the season. Some had said that, in his midthirties, Joe D was in decline. His answer was to lead his team with a .346 average. It was the Yankees' 16th pennant and the first season for their new manager, former Dodger Casey Stengel.

As usual, New Yorkers stopped dead in their tracks during the first week of October 1949. Primitive black-and-white TVs were gaining in popularity, but radio was still king. In schools, shops, train stations, garages, offices, and even certain churches, everyone had his or her ear glued to a station. If you were a Dodger fan, you listened to the mellow sound of Red Barber; if you rooted for the Yankees, you followed the gospel according to Mel Allen. Ironically, in a city infamous for extreme urban accents, New Yorkers took to two Southerners with decidedly Dixie drawls: Red was from Mississippi, Mel from Alabama.

Newk deservedly got the nod for game one, at the Stadium. His rookie year had been sensational. And so was his performance in game one. In eight innings, he didn't walk a soul, didn't allow a run, and fanned 11. The problem was, Allie Reynolds was pitching just as well. When the Yankees came to bat in the bottom of the ninth, there was no score—that is, until Tommy Henrich led off the inning with a game-winning homer to right.

Yanks 1, Bums 0.

Game two, at the Stadium, was another thrilling pitchers' duel—Preacher Roe versus Vic Raschi. In the second inning we drew first blood when Jackie doubled and Hodges singled him home. Roe shut out the Yankees and this time we won 1–0.

Yanks 1, Bums 1—and we're going home to Brooklyn.

I started game three in Ebbets Field.

"Are you nervous?" Ann had asked me the night before.

"More eager than nervous," I said. "I like playing in the big games."

"You like pressure?"

"I like getting to prove myself."

"Well, you've already proven yourself to me and my family—so you haven't anything else to prove."

"I have a game to win," I said.

That game went according to plan. My confidence was high. I'd won my last 14 appearances in Ebbets Field. My fastball was hopping, and I pitched eight strong innings, giving up just two hits and a run. At one point I'd retired 14 straight.

Our bats were quiet that day. Pee Wee's solo shot in the fourth tied the game. Going into the top of the ninth I was still on the mound and we were still tied 1–1.

I got Henrich to ground out but then walked Yogi. Joe D popped out in foul territory. Two outs, one on. Then Bobby Brown singled to right and I walked Gene Woodling. Bases loaded. Stengel called back Cliff Mapes from the on-deck circle and put in a pinch hitter instead. Johnny Mize grabbed a bat and approached the plate.

Johnny was a left-handed .260 hitter that year, but his lifetime average would settle at the .312 mark. I was concerned, of course, because I had men on every base, but not especially worried about Johnny. Coach Clyde Sukeforth came out to talk to me. Old man Shotton in street clothes, you'll remember, never walked to the mound. Campy joined our huddle along with Jackie and Pee Wee.

"What do you think, Ralphie?" asked Clyde.

"I think I have to get this son of a bitch out."

"You tired?" Clyde wanted to know.

"No," I answered honestly.

"Is he throwing like he's tired?" Clyde asked Campy.

"No," said Campy.

"Then we're gonna stick with you, Ralph," Clyde decided. "It's your game to win."

What happened was a battle royal. It was one of those at-bats in which you don't think there will ever be a resolution. I kept giving him good stuff and he kept fouling it off. The count was 1–2 and after another five or six pitches it was still 1–2. I threw a fastball up and in and a slider down and in and he kept fouling them off. Finally, on a high, tight fastball, he threw the head of the bat around and hit a ball off the right-field wall, scoring two runs. They took me out and replaced me with Jack Banta to face Jerry Coleman. Banta hung a curve and Coleman blooped one to center field, scoring another run—which proved to be the winning run.

In the bottom of the ninth, Luis Olmo and Bruce Edwards both walloped solo shots, but that was it. We went down 4–3 and the Yankees went up two games to one.

The next day, a Saturday, was not Newk's day. In his second start, big Don gave up a walk and three doubles in the top of the fourth. The Yanks got three more off reliever Joe Hatten in the fifth and went on to win 6–4.

New York led three games to one.

Sunday afternoon at Ebbets Field. If the Yanks prevailed, that would mean getting swept at home and losing the Series. We couldn't let that happen.

Shotton started Rex Barney (9–8, ERA 4.41) against Vic Raschi (21–10, ERA, 3.34). It was a slugfest. After 22 hits and 16 runs, the Yankees wound up ahead, 10–6, and were world champions.

Wait till next year.

"How are you feeling?" Ann asked the next day.

"I'm not jumping for joy, but I'll be all right."

We were sitting around the Mulvey kitchen table—Ann, myself, and her mom and dad.

The coffee was good and strong, but the silence was even stronger. No one knew exactly what to say. Finally, Dearie, a vociferous fan, voiced what we were all thinking.

"Wait till next year."

When I went home to Mount Vernon, my parents, brothers, and sisters couldn't have been more encouraging about my appearance in game three.

"Hell," said brother John, "you pitched eight and two-thirds great innings."

"Well, eight great innings anyway."

"You nearly got Mize."

"Give Mize credit," I said. "He had staying power."

"Could have gone either way," said John.

"Wuddas, cuddas, and shuddas will drive a man crazy," I said.

"You're right," John agreed. "But there's no reason not to hold your head high."

That winter I had time to think over the '49 season. Maybe we pitchers think too much—and particularly think too much about our pitching arms. We worry about them. We cover them, soak them, rub them, pamper them, get them massaged and examined regularly. And we get paranoid about them.

As the forties gave way to the fifties, I took stock of my arm. Since the unfortunate infection in 1948, it clearly had not been the same. The 1949 season started off great. The fact that I won only three games after the break had me realizing that, although I'd refused to admit it, soreness had returned, keeping me from throwing with my usual velocity.

I monitored that soreness as the Dodgers barnstormed through Mexico, Texas, Oklahoma, Louisiana, and Alabama. We faced all sorts of opponents, some polished, some raggedy. For the most part

Mr. Ralph Branca
522 So. 9th ave
Mt. Vernon. N.Y.

March   , 1943

Dear Sir:

Your name is carried on our records as a young man who is desirous of becoming a professional baseball player. This year, baseball offers opportunities that have not been available to the inexperienced player in previous years.

Due to so many players in our organization entering the armed forces, there is a definite scarcity of players in the lower leagues. We are offering tryouts to youngsters below the draft age and those that have not been called or are deferred for some reason.

We are planning to have a series of tryouts at Ebbets Field, or some other centrally located spot in Brooklyn, prior to the opening of our regular minor league training camps this season. Boys selected at that camp will be sent to spring training at our expense.

We feel that this affords a splendid opportunity for the ambitious youngster to determine whether or not he has the ability to become a professional baseball player. Competent scouts and coaches will be present at these sessions to pass judgment on the abilities of the players.

If you are interested in this opportunity, please let me hear from you at your earliest convenience.

Very truly yours,

Branch Rickey, Jr.

The invitation that changed my life.

My brother John, a great pitcher in his own right.

Number 13 and a black cat. I still wasn't superstitious. April 1951. (*Courtesy of Bettman/Corbis*)

September 1947. I'd just beaten the Cards. *From left:* Hank Behrman, Jackie Robinson, Cookie Lavagetto, and me. (*Courtesy of Bettman/Corbis*)

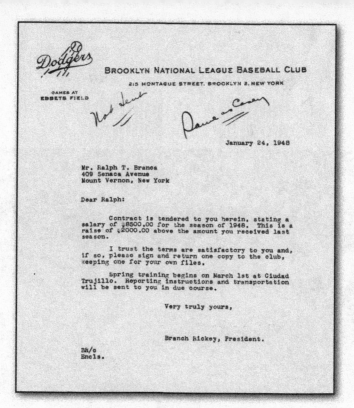

Rickey reluctantly reaches into his wallet.

Young fans in Vero Beach. February 1951.
(*Courtesy of Bettman/Corbis*)

Hawk, big number 13, the early fifties.
(*Courtesy of Bettman/Corbis*)

October 3, 1951. The aftermath. I head to the clubhouse. Jackie stands in disbelief. *(Courtesy of Bettman/Corbis)*

October 3, 1951. On the clubhouse steps, I'm inconsolable.
(*Courtesy of Getty Images*)

All in fun. I'm choking Bobby Thomson during the 1951 Giants/Yankees World Series. *(Courtesy of Bettman/Corbis)*

The pitching staff surrounding Campy, Vero Beach, 1952. *From left:* me, Carl Erskine, Preacher Roe, Clem Labine. *(Courtesy of Bettman/Corbis)*

A Tiger in Yankee Stadium, 1953.
(Courtesy of Bettman/Corbis)

A Yankee in Yankee Stadium,
1954. *(Courtesy of Getty Images)*

Ralph Branca Day, Mt. Vernon, 1969. *From left:* Bill Branca, me, and the son of Muhammad Gado Nasko, consul general from Nigeria.

Jackie Robinson's funeral, October 27, 1972. Carrying the casket, *on left*: Bill Russell and me; *on right*: Don Newcombe and Pee Wee Reese. Campy watches from his wheelchair. *(Courtesy of Bettman/Corbis)*

My wonderful brother John Branca (wearing glasses), New York State assemblyman, chairman of the New York State Athletic Commission, 1983.

With my friend Bobby Thomson (wearing glasses), 1991. *(Courtesy of Getty Images)*

it was a good way to keep in shape. But as I pitched, even on days when I was effective, I felt a strain.

I kept it a secret. I was careful not to overexert myself, but I was not about to complain or even remotely hint that something was wrong with me. I was going to tough it out. Injuries—especially muscular aches and pains—have a way of healing themselves. Sometimes it's just a question of time. Sometimes the best we can do is nothing. That was my line of thinking. Ignore it and it'll go away. Be positive. And whatever you do, don't give the coaches a reason to bench you.

That winter, our first in the new spring training facility in Vero Beach, Florida, I thought of nothing but the future and wished my soreness away.

The future of the Dodgers was radically altered in 1950 when Walter O'Malley took charge by pushing Branch Rickey out. The story was this:

Dodger ownership in 1950 was divided four ways—Rickey; a businessman named John Smith; Ann's mom, Dearie; and O'Malley, team vice president and chief counsel. After O'Malley bought Smith's share, he strengthened his position. He didn't like the way Rickey was running the team and was prepared to buy his shares and give him the boot. Anticipating his removal, Rickey made a slick move. He gave Bill Zeckendorf, the real estate mogul, a $50,000 fee to buy his share of the team for more than $1 million, a huge amount in those days. If O'Malley wanted control, he had no choice but to buy the shares from Zeckendorf, who returned Rickey's fee. Rickey was out, but even richer. The Pirates hired him immediately as their GM. O'Malley was angry to pay an inflated price. But O'Malley got what he wanted—total control.

The guy most concerned about the move was Jackie Robinson.

Jackie and Rickey had a bond. After all, were it not for Rickey, Jackie might not have had his tremendous place in history.

"He's my guy," Jackie told me during spring training. "He's one of the greatest men I've ever known. I don't know this O'Malley."

"I've heard he's okay."

"You hear that from your girlfriend's parents?"

"From a lot of people. He's smart and willing to put some money into the team. Rickey's a skinflint."

"He was fair with me."

"I understand that, Jackie, and no one's gonna forget how he brought you up. Ultimately, though, you made your own mark. You're the guy—not Branch Rickey—who got the hits, made the catches, and ran the bases."

"I don't know, Ralph, I feel kind of vulnerable without knowing Rickey's in my corner."

"Didn't you say that Rickey demanded that you bite your tongue for the first three years? Well, those three years are gone and so is Rickey. You can say what you want and be who you are. You can tell those umps where they can go—especially the ones who haven't been giving you the calls. Rickey liked you, but that didn't keep him from low-balling you when it came to money. I have a feeling that O'Malley's someone who puts his money where his mouth is. You got a raise, didn't you?"

"I did."

"That's great. You deserve it. And, given how you're going to play next year, you'll still be underpaid."

At $35,000, Jackie was.

He was also free to finally be himself. If he wanted to lash back at opposing players and managers calling him names, he could lash back. And he did. And it did us all good to see him finally stand up for himself.

It's interesting that one of his biggest tormentors was Durocher. The two of them were oil and water. Jackie never forgot how Leo had publicly teased him for being overweight back during spring training of '48. I also think Leo knew that Jackie was the key to the Giants beating us. If Durocher could rattle Jackie's cage, maybe he could upset the whole team.

I remembered something Leo, then still the Dodger manager, had told me when he was on Jackie's case for being too fat.

"Robinson is too sensitive," said Leo. "He needs a thicker skin."

"Maybe you need to go easy on him," I said. "He's had to take a lot of shit."

"Go easy on him? Are you kidding, Branca? I ain't going easy on anyone. The easier you go, the faster you lose."

Whatever else happened to the Dodgers in 1950, Jackie had another great season, playing in his second of what would be six consecutive All-Star games and hitting .328.

As the start of the season neared, on a modest scale, I was getting some notice. I hired Frank Scott, who may have been the first sports agent in baseball history. If entertainers had agents, I didn't see why athletes couldn't have them as well. After all, as earners we had an extremely limited run. We were handcuffed by the brutally restrictive reserve clause. We lacked leverage. Most of us weren't trained to do much else but play ball, so why not be smart and make money while we could? Scott got on the case. He secured me a Wheaties endorsement and put me in ads for Buster Brown shoes. I also recorded a song called "Brooklyn Dodgers Jump," accompanied by my teammates Erv Palica and Carl Furillo.

My teammates also got on me for dating Ann.

"Hey, Ralph," Tommy Brown teased, "trying to move up in the world? I hear you're dating O'Malley's daughter."

"No, Tommy, I'm not dating O'Malley's daughter. I don't know O'Malley's daughter."

"You calling me a liar?"

"I'm calling you misinformed. I'm dating Ann Mulvey."

"Who's she?"

"The daughter of Jim and Dearie Mulvey."

"Aren't they owners?"

"Dearie is a part owner."

"So I'm right. You're trying to climb up the social ladder."

"If there is a social ladder, I'm about to grab it and bust it over your head."

Other guys, whom I liked more than Tommy, also gave me a hard time.

Furillo said, "The thing is, Ralph, if Shotton won't start you, you can always call your girlfriend's mother."

More sensitive guys such as Reese, Robinson, Newk, Oisk, and Duke didn't say a word. They knew Ann was a class act, and they were happy for me.

At about this time, Vince Scully joined the Dodger broadcast team. Scully grew up in the Polo Grounds cheering Mel Ott just like I did. Two years younger than I, Vinnie went to Fordham and developed an encyclopedic knowledge of baseball. His boss, Red Barber, told his announcers not to socialize with the players. But I convinced Scully to meet Ann's roommate at Marymount. We double-dated, and Vinnie and I became lifelong friends.

In the summer of 1950, with news of a pending war in Korea in all the papers, we set out to repeat our pennant victory and, once again, try to break Brooklyn's World Series jinx. On June 28, the day President Truman commanded naval and air forces to fight on the side of South Korea, the Dodgers were clinging to a half-game first-place lead over the Phils and Cards. The team was doing okay. I wasn't.

More than at any point in my career, I was struggling. I was 2–3 and my ERA had ballooned to 6.07. I wound up the year at 7–9, and worked my ERA down to 4.69, but I was still suffering. My arm wasn't right. The only bright spot was my work in relief.

In the last half of the season my ERA as a reliever was 3.50. As a starter I gave up 21 homers in 94 innings, but as a reliever, in 21 innings, I allowed only 3.

It felt good to be able to help my team in the stretch of another thrilling pennant race. I was in the bullpen every day as the closer. That meant I threw every day. My arm was regaining its strength, and I was soon back to my '47 form.

Before I tell the story of that race, I need to make another old-timer observation:

I understand the commercial value of the multitiered playoff system. I know you can't argue with revenue. The money made from a month of playoff games is enormous. Since the paradigm was established in 1969, divisional playoff and league championship games have created many a beautiful memory for fans. I've enjoyed watching many of those games myself. But . . .

There is beauty in simplicity. In the forties and fifties, we played only those teams in our league; whoever came out on top after a full season won the pennant and went to the Series. I loved how that worked. It was direct. It was definitive. It represented a lot of hard work and consistency over a long period of time, and it was often thrilling. In a close race, elimination was quick and absolute. Two league winners, one world champion.

In 1950 we were three games out, behind the great Philadelphia Whiz Kids team of Andy Seminick, Richie Ashburn, Del Ennis, and Dick Sisler. Their pitching staff—led by Robin Roberts, Curt Simmons, and Jim Konstanty—was among the best in either league.

On August 15, they increased their lead to six-and-a-half games.

On September 5, they were seven ahead.

On September 15, when they moved seven and a half ahead with a little more than two weeks left in the season, it looked hopeless. Except we didn't lose hope—which is when the Phillies started losing games and we started winning.

When Philly came into Ebbets Field on September 30, for the final two games of the year, we had closed the gap to two games. If we could win these next two, we'd wind up dead even and force a playoff.

On that Saturday afternoon, Erv Palica pitched a complete game. Campy and Duke each hit his 31st homer, and we won 7–3. On Sunday, all the marbles would be on the table.

Sunday was another pitchers' duel—Robin Roberts for them, Big Newk for us. The temperature was unseasonably hot—it felt like mid-July—but Don was on. He was after his 20th victory and the most important win of his young career. He pitched beautifully, giving up only one run in nine innings.

In the bottom of the ninth, when the score was tied 1–1, it looked like we had them. Sweet victory was in our grasp. Roberts, who had pitched as well as Newk—Reese's homer in the sixth was his only mistake—walked Cal Abrams. Reese singled. Man on first, winning run at second in the person of Cal Abrams, no outs. Duke at the plate. Duke might have bunted both runners over except for two reasons: he was a bad bunter, and Roberts was expert at breaking up bunt attempts. Rather than sacrifice, Duke swung away and connected. It was a line-drive single to center!

Cal, a slow runner, was bluffed back to second base before taking a wide turn at third.

Richie Ashburn, the Phils' center fielder, shallow in case of a wild pickoff throw, grabbed the ball.

Third-base coach Milt Stock waved Cal home.

No! Don't do that! Ashburn has him beat on the play! Stop Cal at third!

But it was too late, Cal came running to the plate, where catcher Stan Lopata—a big man at 6'2" and 210 pounds—had the ball firmly in his mitt. Abrams, unable to dislodge Lopata, was out by a mile.

Everyone on the bench was thinking the same thing: *not only should Stock have kept Cal at third, but, even more pointedly, Shotton should have removed Cal for pinch runner Ed Miksis.* Miksis was a speed demon. Miksis was the guy who, back in game four of the '47 World Series with the Yanks, pinch-ran for Reiser, taking off after Cookie Lavagetto's double and scoring all the way from first base to win the game. If Shotton had put in Eddie for Abrams, we would have won.

But Shotton wasn't worried; he was too busy keeping his box score nice and tidy.

After Cal got nailed, Roberts walked Jackie intentionally to load the bases again. We had two more great chances to score—Furillo and Hodges. A hit by either man meant that our miraculous comeback would be realized.

Both men flew out.

Frustration set in.

Going into the top of the tenth, we were tied 1–1.

Robin Roberts singled off Newk. Then Eddie Waitkus singled to center. Two on, no outs. Ashburn's sacrifice moved the runners over. Men on second and third, one out. Dick Sisler at the plate.

Sisler was the son of George Sisler, the famous first baseman for the St. Louis Browns, who held the record for the most hits (257) in a single season (1920). (In 2004, Ichiro Suzuki of the Seattle Mariners broke that record with 262 hits.) In 1950, Dick Sisler had strong numbers himself—hitting .296 with a dozen homers and 80 RBIs.

Shouldn't Shotton have ordered Newk to walk Sisler and set up a force at every base? He decided not to.

Shouldn't Shotton have relieved Newk who, after 125 pitches, was feeling the strain? No, Shotton didn't think that was a good idea.

Sisler got all of Newk's fastball, lifting it high into the left-field stands. Three runs scored. Phils 4, Bums 1.

We went down 1–2–3 in the tenth, and the Phillies won the pennant.

In the clubhouse, Newk was crushed.

"You pitched a hell of a game, big guy," I said. "You got nothing to be ashamed of."

"I cost us the pennant."

"What are you talking about? We got this close because of you. And besides, they only got you one run today. If they'd given you more to work with, you'd be the hero."

"I feel like a chump."

"You're a champ, Newk, not a chump," I said. "We'll get 'em next year."

That off-season, Cal Abrams went to work, as he had done before, pumping gas at $150 a week. Many of the guys had menial off-season jobs to keep their heads above water. Milt Stock was fired for waving Cal home. The guy who should have been fired was Burt Shotton—and he was, but not until spring training of 1951, the year that would lead to a moment in time unlike any other.

In the Year of Our Lord
Nineteen-Hundred Fifty-one

IBELIEVE IN GOD. I've always believed in God. As a child, I
saw God in the eyes of my mother. She was incapable of not
loving her children, just as I was told God was incapable of
not loving His. My father was the same, a man devoted to love. My
brothers and sisters devoted their lives to supporting one another.
All this was based on the premise that God had created us for
the purpose of demonstrating His love through acts of kindness,
understanding, and grace.

The God I worshiped—and worship today—is not interested
in who wins or loses a baseball game. At least that's my view of
God. His concern is with our hearts. He wants our hearts to widen
in empathy and deepen in generosity.

But competitive athletes are a strange breed. Some are convinced that God is on their side; that God is really a Dodger fan
or a Giant fan. Competition can make us a little crazy. Obsessive
competitiveness is part of the emotional package of being great in
sports. You have to hate losing with a vengeance. You have to love
winning with a passion. The need to excel on the field can throw
us off-balance. Obsessions can throw anyone off-balance.

Charlie Dressen, the new Dodger manager who took over in 1951, had an obsession: Leo Durocher. Shotton was fired by O'Malley because Shotton was Rickey's man. O'Malley was so interested in wiping out Rickey's legacy that anyone in the front office mentioning Branch's name was fined a buck. Dressen had had practically no relationship with Rickey, but, man, did he have a relationship with Leo!

Durocher was a star. Like Casey Stengel and Joe McCarthy, he'll be forever remembered as one of the great baseball minds. Dressen came up under Durocher. He was one of his minions. As Leo commanded the stage and demanded the spotlight, Dressen suffered in the shadows. Dressen wanted to be as smart as Durocher. He wanted to be as famous. And when he was named Dodger manager, his driving goal was not to beat the Giants, but to beat Leo. Day in and day out, you'd see Charlie walking up and down the dugout, looking at the scoreboard, looking to see how the Giants were doing in their games against Pittsburgh or Cincy or Philly. If they were winning, you'd hear him mutter to himself, "That friggin' Durocher!"

Getting back to God:

I don't believe that God directs the outcome of baseball games, but I do believe that He directs us in matters of love. I believe I was directed to woo and win the favor of Ann and, as best I could, convince her to be my wife. When I proposed in November of 1950, she said, "Before I give you my answer, let's see what kind of season you have."

The Mulveys had a great sense of humor, but part of me was afraid that Ann was only half-kidding.

"Of course I'll marry you, Ralph Branca. I've been in love with you before I knew what love is."

"What will your father say?"

"You're going to have to find out for yourself."

I called Mr. Mulvey to ask whether I could speak with him in private.

"Sure, Ralph," he said. "Come by the house tonight."

When I arrived, Ann and her mom had gone out for the evening, leaving the men to their business.

"Have a seat," he said, as I followed him into the den. His desk was piled high with papers.

"How's the movie business?" I asked.

"We're worried about TV taking over."

"Will it?"

"Probably—at least for a while. But people are always going to want to get out of the house and sit in a theater to watch a film. It's a community event. It's a ritual. Television is a marvelous invention, and I'm sure that after television some other marvelous viewing invention will come along. One day we'll probably be able to watch movies on our wristwatches. But a beautiful theater with a big screen will always draw customers. Movies will always be around. But something tells me you didn't come over here to discuss movies."

"No, sir."

"Yesterday I was 'Jim,'" he said. "Today I'm 'sir.'"

"You know why I'm here."

"If it's to use my influence with O'Malley to get you a raise, you've come to the wrong person. Dearie is the one with the clout."

"I'd never ask anything like that of either you or Dearie."

"We know that, Ralph; we just like to kid."

"I've come to ask you for your daughter's hand in marriage."

"And I'd like to give you both my blessing."

"Wow. I didn't think it would be this easy."

"It's going to be even easier. Name the date and Dearie and I will throw the party."

"We're thinking late October."

"After another subway Series with the Yankees?"

"After the Dodgers' first World Championship."

"That should put the icing on the cake. I'm looking for your best season ever, Ralph."

"With a happy ending like this, I can't wait to get out to the mound. I don't anticipate any problems."

I'd been great in '47, but four years had passed. I was stronger and more experienced in '51. The soreness was gone, and my motivation was sky high. Motivation was sky high for all the Dodgers.

Our frustrations had mounted:

In '46, we tied the Cards for first place but got beaten in the postseason playoff, the first in history.

In '47, we won the pennant but got beaten by the Yanks in the seven-game World Series.

In '49, we didn't clinch the pennant till October 3, barely squeaking by the Cards, only to get beaten 4–1 by the Yankees in the Series.

In '50, we could have—should have—beat the Phils on the last day of the regular season to force a playoff, but we didn't.

Now, '51. Down to a man, we Dodgers knew that '51 was going to be our year.

A week before Opening Day, Harry Truman sacked Douglas MacArthur. In the president's words, the general was "unable to support the policies of the United States." Our spanking new manager, Charlie Dressen, took the occasion to remind us that he, too, would not tolerate insubordination.

"This is a new regime," he told the team. "Forget how you played under Durocher. Forget how you played under Shotton. These are going to be the Dressen years—and don't you ever forget it."

I also don't think Dressen ever forgot that moment back in '46 when I, an insubordinate, told him that I couldn't make any friggin' money pitching batting practice. Not then, not ever, was I on Dressen's list of favorites. I imagine that Dressen might have been disappointed when two years earlier Leo hadn't been able to trade me for Bobby Thomson. At best, my relationship with Charlie was frosty. I suspected he knew that I knew Leo was a far superior strategist.

Whether I liked Dressen or not, this was my eighth season as a Dodger and I was as determined as any of my teammates to bring home the championship. This was also my sixth year acting as team rep. The issues might seem trivial compared to the high-finance leverage of ballplayers today, but we wanted every team to put two mounds in the bullpen so two pitchers could be warming up at the same time.

I had another duty as team rep. It might have been overly optimistic on my part, but I initiated discussions about the possibility of receiving World Series money. *If we win this year, do we take that income and put it in a pension fund, or do we simply divide it up?* I was introducing the team to more sophisticated financial options. I had no idea at the time, but this was a precursor of my post-baseball life. My supplementary income—from being on baseball cards and appearing in ads—was marginal, so the World Series money, if there was to be any, had great significance.

I overcame pneumonia in spring training and was ready to go. While the rest of the country was tuning into Senator Estes Kefauver's public hearings on organized crime—some call it the first major news drama played out on TV—the '51 baseball season got under way. No one had an inkling that we were about to live through the most thrilling six months in the history of the sport.

My first appearance of the year would be—you guessed it—in the Polo Grounds, the same ballpark where, some six months later, I would make my last appearance of the year. Newcombe had beaten the Giants the day before, 7–3; I beat them by the same score on April 21; and the next day Newcombe got the win in relief. We had faced their best pitchers—Sal Maglie, Johnny Sain, and Sheldon Jones—and mowed them down three straight, a helluva omen for the rest of the season. We felt that our pitching staff—Preacher Roe, Newk, Oisk, Clyde King, Clem Labine, and yours truly—was the best in both leagues.

After that initial sweep of the Giants, Dressen was beside himself. He was acting like we had already won the pennant.

"Did you see that expression on Leo's face?" he asked me after the third game. "He looked like he lost his best friend. He did—*me*. By the time this year is over, Durocher is gonna be begging for mercy. Hey, boys, let's go give him a little serenade."

I wouldn't go—that's not my style—but Charlie recruited a couple of Dodgers to help him taunt Leo and his Giants as they sang outside their dressing room, "The Giants is dead! The Giants is dead!"

I didn't pitch again until May 1, and then in relief. For reasons I didn't understand, Dressen decided I was more a reliever than a starter. Fine. Anything to help us get to the World Series.

Sunday, May 20, was a scary day. Jackie had received a death threat. The cops and a local newspaper in Cincy had received letters saying someone was going to shoot him during our doubleheader at Crosley Field. The FBI suggested that Jackie not play. Jackie wouldn't hear of it.

"The threat's a bluff," he said. "They just don't want us to win. If I heeded every threat, I'd wind up sitting on the bench all year."

Jackie played. And how! In the seventh inning of the first game, Ewell Blackwell walked Duke to get to Jackie, who promptly powered a mighty shot over the center-field fence. Even the Cincy fans cheered the man. We also won the second game. In the two games, inspired by Jackie's courage, we scored 24 runs.

Jackie's new approach that began in '50 really flourished in '51. He was now a free and feisty competitive athlete. Some said he was getting headstrong and arrogant, but I didn't see him that way. He was expressing his true nature, a guy not about to be disrespected by anyone. This was the Jackie I liked best.

On May 26, I had four strikeouts in two shutout innings against the Braves. My ERA was 1.40.

Dressen awarded me a couple of days later by starting me against the Phils. In the eighth inning I was hanging tough in a 3–3 tie when the clouds cracked open and rain soaked Shibe Park. The delay lasted an hour. I was so sure I'd be yanked for a reliever, I'd taken a shower and changed clothes. Then the word came down—I was to complete the game. Furillo's homer in the top of the ninth gave us the win. Next day, a headline read: BRANCA RELIEVES BRANCA FOR BROOKLYN WIN!

I had five starts in a row, pitched four complete games, and won them all. In the fifth game, I was losing 1–0 when I was taken out after seven innings for a pinch hitter. I had pitched 43 of a possible 45 innings.

By the end of May, we were in first place, a couple of games ahead of the Cards. We hadn't yet made our big push. The Phils came to Brooklyn. The Phils, you'll remember, never loved Jackie Robinson. In the bottom of the eighth, Jackie singled, stole second, and took third on a wild pitch and was headed home when the Phils thought they had him trapped in a rundown. Not Jackie. When pitcher Russ Meyer came to cover home, Jackie came barreling into him and knocked the ball out of his hand. Safe! Meyer, though, called Jackie every nasty name under the sun. Jackie ignored him and went back to the dugout. But when Meyer threw down the gauntlet and challenged Jackie to fight him right there and then, Jackie bolted out of the dugout. We had to hold him back. Much to Meyer's credit, he apologized to Jackie after the game, and Jackie, ever the gentleman, graciously forgave him the harsh words.

By the middle of June, we had started to move away from the pack and were leading the second-place Giants by six. Meanwhile, Buzzy Bavasi, in his first year as the O'Malley-appointed general manager, had somehow finagled Frankie Frisch, the Cub skipper, to give us left fielder Andy Pafko for Gene Hermanski and Ed Miksis. In 1950, Pafko had hit .304 and 36 homers; he was a superb addition to our team, and the press called the trade "the Big Steal."

The trade also added fuel to the Dressen/Durocher feud. Leo had wanted Pafko and thought Frisch, his old friend and one-time Gashouse Gang manager, was going to hand him over to the Giants. But Dressen had gotten Bavasi to step in before Durocher had a chance. Leo was furious, and Dressen was giddy with delight.

At the beginning of July, the Giants had cut our lead to four and a half games, and I was getting uneasy. I was remembering 1946, when an early July lead of seven and a half games hadn't been enough; by the end of the season the Cards had caught us and then beaten us in the playoffs.

But the Fourth of July was an especially happy holiday for us. We won both ends of a doubleheader against the Giants in Ebbets Field—I pitched the second game and won it 4–2—moving us six and a half games ahead.

After the game Dressen once again led a group of Dodgers in taunting the Giants with his singsong anthem, "The Giants is Dead! The Giants is Dead!"

"I see you're not participating in the sing-along," said Jackie, noticing my boycott.

"It's too soon," I said.

"And bad politics," added Jackie. "If a snake is sleeping, you don't poke him."

"Besides," I said, "it's not about the Dodgers and the Giants. It's about Charlie and Leo. Charlie isn't managing against the Giants. He's managing against Leo. He sees this as his chance to knock out the champ."

"Let's just hope he does," said Jackie.

"Well, so far, so good."

By July 8, we increased our lead to eight and a half games. And at the All-Star break, we were looking good. For my part, I was 7–2. My ERA had risen, but was still among the best in both leagues at 2.27. My arm felt stronger than any time since '47.

Dressen continued to act erratically. On July 18 in Ebbets Field, he brought in Erv Palica with the Pirates ahead 10–5. In five innings of relief Erv gave up three runs and Pittsburgh went on to win 13–12. You would have thought Erv had committed a felony. Charlie chastised him in front of the press, insulting his character as well as his skills. He made Erv feel like the lowliest loser in the world. So vicious was his attack that, after reading Dressen's tirade in the paper, O'Malley called Charlie to his office.

I was in the clubhouse when Pee Wee asked Dressen what O'Malley had said.

"To take it easy on the players," Dressen admitted. "But I said, 'Mr. O'Malley, I hear what you're saying, but is Leo taking it easy on his players? Not for a goddamn minute. Leo is out to get us— and we better as hell understand who we're up against. If we're having a winning year, it's because my strategy is working better than any Dodger manager before, and that includes Shotton and Durocher. Let me run this team and by the time this season's over I'll bring you Leo's head on a silver platter.'"

Now remember this date: *July 19, 1951.*

We were in first place. The Giants and the Cards were tied for second, eight games behind.

Things were shifting behind the scenes. Something was rotten in the state of Denmark. I didn't know it at the time—it would be a few years before I'd learn the truth—but what should have been an even playing field was surreptitiously being tilted to one side.

Oblivious to the mischief being perpetrated in darkened rooms, come August we were riding high. We swept the Giants in a three-game series in Ebbets Field and moved 12½ games ahead of them. For the third time, Dressen led his choir of taunters after the game. The mantra was the same: "The Giants Is Dead!"

The high point came on August 11. In the first game of a dou-bleheader I beat Warren Spahn and the Braves 8–1 for my 10th victory. That put us up 13½ games over the Giants. Even Walter O'Malley started discussing World Series tickets. If the demand was too great he was considering playing our home games in Yankee Stadium to accommodate our fans. I'm not sure he meant that, but the scheme sounded crazy to me.

In the midst of the season, Dearie Mulvey was helping Ann plan our wedding. The date was set—October 20, just after the World Series we hoped to win.

The ceremony would take place at St. Francis Church, just two blocks from the Mulvey home on Maple Street. Invitations went out to 600 guests. Every last relative of my large family would be there along with a huge contingency invited by the Mulveys, a list that included baseball royalty and political big shots. For the dinner and dance, the Mulveys had rented the grand ballroom at the St. George Hotel, a historical landmark in the Brooklyn Heights section of the borough. It was going to be a beautiful affair, the culmination of a beautiful year.

"Don't be concerned about these wedding details," Ann said to me on our way to the Polo Grounds to face the Giants. "You just concentrate on getting the ball over the plate, darling. The wedding will take care of itself."

"What's in that huge shopping bag, Ann?"

"Invitations. I'm going to address them."

"And watch the game at the same time?"

"If you can get your fastball past this rookie Willie Mays, I can certainly address envelopes *and* watch the game at the same time."

On August 14, Erv Palica was scheduled to pitch the first game against New York. He told me he had a sore arm.

"How sore?" I asked.

"Real sore," he answered.

"Tell Charlie. If it's that sore, you shouldn't be pitching."

He told Charlie, who told Erv that it was all in his head.

A few minutes later I saw Erv soaking his arm in the whirlpool.

"That's a waste of time, Irv," I said. "If Charlie's right, you should be soaking your head."

Erv laughed, and then went out and got beaten 4–2.

"Giants just won their fourth in a row," said Hodges after the game.

"Not to worry, Gilly," I said. "I'll get 'em tomorrow."

On August 15, I had my stuff. Through seven innings, we were tied 1–1. In the top of the eighth, Cox doubled and I singled him to third. I felt that he should have scored. This became a key play. Next Furillo drove a clean shot to right-center. A sure hit and a sure run. Except that Willie Mays made the catch of a lifetime and, spinning around, somehow balanced his body and threw a bullet to catcher Wes Westrum. Cox made a hook slide into home but Westrum, blocking the plate, was waiting for him. Double play. No wonder Willie was Rookie of the Year. After the game Jackie, who had made some unbelievable plays in his day, said he'd never seen one that good.

Next inning, Mays led off. It's one of those odd phenomena in baseball: players always seem to come to bat right after a great play in the field. I walked him and then served up a homer to Westrum, who was usually hapless against me and Newk. We lost 3–1.

In the last game of the series, our bats stayed silent and Big Don got beaten 2–1. But when the dust settled, we were still nine and a half ahead. No reason to panic, and yet Dressen was acting like Chicken Little.

"Lose another series like this and we're dead meat!" he screamed. "Dead meat! Do you hear me? You pitchers are slacking off. You bastards think you need more rest than you really do. You're spoiled rotten. The more you pitch, the stronger you get. I ain't about to pamper anyone on this team."

The upshot was that Charlie, in panic mode, began using me and Newk all the time—for both starts and relief.

As the Giants went on a 16-game winning streak that wouldn't end until August 28, our lead was eroding.

On August 24, when I shut out the Cubs on three hits at Ebbets Field, we were down to a seven-and-a-half-game lead. Three days later, I was pitching the first game of a twi-night doubleheader. That's a pitcher's dream. The setting sun does wonders to obscure the hitter's field of vision. In the third inning the Pirates were hitless when their pitcher, Mel Queen, smacked a line drive to right field. Furillo got it on a bounce, and Furillo—the Reading Rifle—actually threw Queen out at first! I'd never seen a play like that before. But leave it to Carl. I had a no-hitter going into the ninth, when I shook off catcher Rube Walker, got the ball up, and watched Pete Castiglione single just over Pee Wee's glove. Cat Metkovich followed with a Baltimore chop for a hit. But that was it. I posted a 5–0 two-hit win.

We lost the second game, though, and our lead was down to five. Our lead had been trimmed by eight and a half games in 13 days. The world was closing in on us in ways we couldn't even begin to understand.

In the Year of Our Lord
Nineteen-Hundred Fifty-one,
the Month of September

I N AN IMMORTAL LINE, T. S. Eliot wrote, "April is the cruelest month."

I'm not in a position to argue with a Nobel Prize–winning poet, but I take exception: September is the cruelest month, and, more specifically, September 1951.

Other than that torrid National League pennant race, the country was relatively normal. Gas cost 19 cents a gallon, the average car set you back $1,500, and you could buy a new three-bedroom house for $9,000. People were going to see Gene Kelly in *An American in Paris*, Humphrey Bogart in *The African Queen*, and newcomer Marlon Brando in *A Streetcar Named Desire*. Hoagy Carmichael was crooning "In the Cool Cool Cool of the Evening" and Billy Eckstine had a hit with "I Apologize."

Tired of the Korean War, some citizens had started an "I Like Ike" bid, hoping to draft the general as the Republican nominee for president in 1952 and end the war. In England they were talking about bringing another war hero, Winston Churchill, back to power.

If you lived in the New York area, though, none of these things held a candle to the drama unfolding between two ballparks, one in upper Manhattan and another in Flatbush.

The Giants were after the Dodgers.

Leo was after Dressen.

Dressen was after Leo.

And I was after Sal "the Barber" Maglie, who was pitching against me at the start of a critical two-game series. With four weeks till the end of the regular season, our first-place lead was seven games, a somewhat comfortable margin. The feeling was— *sweep the Giants now and put them away once and for all.*

As I relive this month, an experience that is equal parts pain and excitement, I don't want to rush the story. I say this because you cannot appreciate the monumental drama of October 3, 1951, without understanding what led to that moment. So get ready for a roller-coaster ride.

September 1

I pitched against the Giants at the Polo Grounds and got bombed, 8–1. Our lead was cut to six. I don't believe I had my best stuff that day, but I do recall Thomson stepping into a perfectly placed curve and hitting his first home run ever against me. I said to myself, "He just outguessed me."

September 2

The Giants also bombed Newk, 11–2. Our lead was cut to five games.

September 8

Newk came back strong and threw a two-hit shutout against the Giants. We won 9–0 and went back up six and a half games. The next day I was home in Mount Vernon reading the morning

130

papers. A writer said that Giant shortstop Alvin Dark and Herman Franks, Leo's bullpen coach and first lieutenant, were snooping around the Dodger dugout after the game looking for wires. They were convinced we had set up some kind of electrical device to steal their signs and call them from the bench. I never heard of something so crazy. If you can steal a sign on the field, fine; but no team uses off-the-field mechanical hookups to read and relay the catcher's signs. That would be blatant cheating. Anyway, Dark and Franks found nothing.

September 9

Capacity crowd at Ebbets Field to see the last Dodger-Giant game of the regular season. I was pitching against the Barber again, and this time really wanted to give him a shave. It was close. The pitchers' duel went to the eighth. I'd given up five hits and two runs. Maglie had a shutout going. But after Pee Wee grounded out, Snider doubled and Jackie tripled him home. Tying run on third. Pafko hit a grounder down the third-base line to Bobby Thomson. I'm not sure why Jackie didn't break for home. Instead he ran back to the bag, where Thomson tagged him and doubled up Andy at first. We lost the game 2–1 while Maglie won his 20th. Our lead was down to five and a half.

After the game, Charlie reverted to panic mode. He rode Jackie hard. Jackie was a brilliant ballplayer and knew he'd made a mistake. He didn't need Dressen to remind him. But Charlie, who loved to credit his strategy when we won and blame his players when we lost, couldn't be contained. "That knucklehead play of yours," he told Jackie, "could cost us the pennant."

September 11

Before the game I told my brother John, "We're in the driver's seat. I still think Dressen's overreacting. He's having nightmares about Leo snagging the pennant on the last day of the season."

"Can't anyone calm him down?" John asked.

"Pee Wee tries, but Charlie's always telling Pee Wee that he's too relaxed. Charlie says tension keeps us on our toes."

Maybe so. Maybe it was tension that led to Clem Labine's six-hit shutout against Cincy. With 14 games to go, we were six up.

September 16

Labine won again, this time 6–1 against the Cubs at Wrigley. But the Giants kept winning as well. They pounded Pittsburgh 7–1. Reading the box score the next day, I noticed that Bobby Thomson hit his 28th home run. Bobby was having a helluva year. Our lead had been dwindling. The Giants were down by only four and a half games.

September 18

The Cards shelled me, 7–1, while Monte Irvin's 22nd homer of the year, a two-run shot, put the Giants over the Reds, 6–5. Our lead decreased to three slim games.

September 19

Our lead increased to three and a half games. The Giants were idle while Preacher Roe, in his 21st win, shut out the Cards 3–0.

September 20

With only 10 games left, the Giants finally lost to the Cubs, Hodges' 39th homer beat the Cards, and we were back to four and a half in front. After the game in our clubhouse in St. Louis, you could hear a collective sigh of relief.

September 21

At the end of our 5–4 road trip, we flew back from Missouri—planes had finally replaced trains for this long trip—arriving just in time to take the field against the Phils. (Those who refused to fly—Billy Cox, Cal Abrams, and Preacher Roe—missed the game because the train was late.) We were feeling as though we could—we had to—regain the momentum.

Every game had become crucial.

Labine started. He had been terrific. In his last four outings, he had pitched four complete-game victories for an ERA of 1.00. In the first inning, though, Clem got into trouble. Two infield hits and a walk loaded the bases. He faced Willie Jones and, following correct protocol, pitched him from a stretch. That's what you do with the bases loaded. Dressen, on the other hand, was signaling for Labine to execute a full windup before throwing the ball. Charlie was wrong, and Clem ignored him. Pitching from a stretch, Labine hung the ball over the plate, and Jones blasted it out for a grand slam. We never recovered. Robin Roberts won his 21st at our expense, 9–6. After the game, Dressen was furious that Clem had refused to wind up. Clem was right, but Charlie couldn't contain his rage, screaming, "You'll be lucky if you see another inning of action this year!"

Clem wasn't in Charlie's doghouse. He was under it.

Our lead dropped back down to four games with nine to go.

The odds favored us.

"You're going to do it," said my future mother-in-law, Dearie Mulvey.

"You're my son," said Mom, "and I have all the faith in the world in you."

"You're my brother," said John, "and you're going to pull this thing off."

My support system was strong as steel. I was feeling good.

September 22

The Saturday opener of our two-game series with the Phils went sour. They beat us 7–3. Over at the Polo Grounds, Larry Jansen got his 20th win, beating Warren Spahn. You'd think the Giant fans would be more into the race, but when I checked the stats I saw that not even 12,000 fans were at the Polo Grounds that day, a park that held 55,000.

It didn't matter. All that counted was that our lead fell to three games.

September 23

On Sunday, Preacher preached a full sermon, completed a six-hitter against the Phils, and boosted his record to 22–2. Up in Manhattan, the Barber also won his 22nd, beating the Braves.

The lead remained at three.

September 24

We were off while the Giants played the Braves. I was listening to Giants announcer Russ Hodges describe the ninth inning with the score tied 3–3 when my old roommate Eddie Stanky singled home the winning run.

Our lead had shrunk to two and a half.

September 25

On the train up to Boston, there wasn't much to discuss. We had a twi-night doubleheader and knew we had to win at least one.

In the first game, I got trounced. We lost 6–3.

In the second game, Oisk got trounced. We lost 14–2.

In Philly, the Giants won their fourth straight, beating Robin Roberts.

Hard to believe, but we were down to a single-game lead.

How in hell could this have happened?

"Doesn't matter," said Jackie, probably the most ferocious competitor among us. "Let's just bear down in these last five games. We control our own fate. We win all five and we win the pennant."

September 26

We did bear down. We bombed the Braves 15–5. It was Newk's 19th win. We were feeling good until we looked over at the scoreboard: Giants 10, Phillies 1.

Our lead was still one.

September 27

The Giants were idle so we could pick up half a game in our final meeting with Boston.

It was a tight, nervous game. Every game was like that now. Bottom of the eighth, 3–3 tie, Braves batting. Preacher, the starter, still pitching.

Bob Addis singled to center. Sam Jethroe singled him to third. Earl Torgeson hit a grounder to Reese, who fired it home. Campy had the plate blocked. He had Addis dead to rights. Made the tag. Not even close. But the ump, Frank Dascoli, blew it—he said Addis averted the tag and called him safe. A photo in the paper the next day would show that Campy had blocked the plate and Addis wasn't within two feet of the plate. Boston 4, Brooklyn 3.

Normally the most levelheaded of men, Campy lost it. He threw his mitt in the air. "If that thing comes down," the ump said, "you're outta here." Campy went crazy. He jumped up and down in a fit of fury. No use. We went down in the top of the ninth. Braves won.

Our lead was a half a game. We were hanging on by a thread.

After the game, in the clubhouse Preacher was so ticked off he practically kicked in the umpires' door. A reporter said Jackie was the one who did the kicking, but the reporter was as blind as the ump who called Addis safe.

September 28

On this Friday, the Giants were idle and we were in Philadelphia.

If we could beat the Phils, we'd be back up by a game.

But if we lost, we'd fall into a tie with only two games left in the regular season.

On Saturday and Sunday, the Giants were scheduled to play the Braves in Boston while we remained in Philly to play our last two.

On Friday, we were looking good. Camp's homer in the fifth, his 32nd, put us up 3–1. Although this was a day when Labine normally would have pitched, Clem was still in Charlie's doghouse. Dressen's grudges exceeded his sense. Oisk was on the mound. Carl gave up a run in the sixth, and then in the eighth a two-run homer to Andy Seminick to tie the score. We didn't score in the ninth. In the bottom half of the inning, though, Willie Jones proved to be our nemesis a second time. His single brought in Richie Ashburn from third and won the game.

Things suddenly got very simple.

After 153 games, the Giants had caught us.

With only one remaining weekend left in the regular season—two games for each team—the deadlock could not have been more deadly.

As I tossed and turned that night in my hotel room in the City of Brotherly Love, I tried to chase away the thought, but I couldn't: on August 11, we were 13½ games ahead.

The wisest veteran on our team, Pee Wee Reese, had made a comment then that I'll never forget: "All we have to do is play .500 ball down the stretch and we'll have it made." Well, we'd done just that. We had played .500. But the Giants had some extra-special ingredient that none of us could understand. They wound up winning 14 of their last 16, and 39 of their last 47. The stats were astounding.

I thought of the next day's games—Newk versus Robin Roberts and, up in Boston, Maglie versus Spahn.

September 29

Campy hit his 33rd homer, Jackie went two for four, and Newk shut out the Braves 5–0.

We did what we had to do.

But so did the Giants. Maglie won his 23rd and beat Spahn 3–0.

Going into the last game of the regular season, the deadlock remained deadly. After 153 games, we were 95 and 58 and so were the Giants.

Over in the American League, the Yankees were in their own tight race with the Indians. Facing the Red Sox in a critical doubleheader, Allie Reynolds hurled his second no-hitter of the year and clinched a pennant tie. Then the Yanks went on to win the second game, nailing their third straight pennant. Man for man, though, I was convinced we had a better team than the Yanks. I saw us beating them in the Series. We just had to get there.

I couldn't sleep. I called Ann.

"Will Dressen pitch Labine tomorrow?" she asked, always the knowledgeable fan.

"Clem should start, but Charlie's still mad. I think he'll go with Preacher."

"Is Preacher tired?" asked my betrothed.

"Honey," I said, "we're all tired."

"You've all comported yourself admirably—especially with this incredible tension. No matter what happens, Ralph, you can't get out of our plans for October 20. The wedding goes on."

"Whose wedding?"

"Very funny."

"I'm going to try and sleep, honey."

"Relax, Ralph, I have a good feeling about tomorrow."

September 30

Sunday. I got up and went to Mass as I usually do. I did not pray for our victory or the Giants' defeat. I thanked God for the gift of my life and for the health of my loved ones. I closed my eyes and concentrated on God's goodness, which had nothing to do with winning or losing sporting events.

The minute I left church, though, I was thinking about the sporting event ahead of me. We had to beat the Phils; the Braves had to beat the Giants. I started to rethink my policy of not asking God to favor one team over another. Maybe I'd make this one exception. But I didn't. I still didn't see God wearing a Dodger cap.

I got to the ballpark. There was silence among the warriors.

Preacher Roe took the mound. I knew Preacher was tired and, sure enough, the Phils got to him in the second inning. By the time I was called in to relieve, they had put four on the board.

In the top of the third, I walked, Furillo singled to left, and Pee Wee tripled me home. Phils 4, Dodgers 1.

It was crunch time.

In the bottom of the third, I got the first two batters, but two walks, a wild pitch, and two singles got the Phillies two more. They led 6–1.

I looked over to the scoreboard and saw that the Giants were beating the Braves in Boston 3–1.

The clock was ticking. Our season was winding down.

In the fourth, Campy's triple resulted in a run. I was taken out for a pinch hitter. Phils 6, Dodgers 2.

We kept fighting. We had to.

In the fifth, Furillo and Reese singled. Then Jackie blasted a towering triple! Carl and Pee Wee scored, and after Pafko singled to right, Jackie came home. We were back in the game. Phils 6, Dodgers 5.

In the bottom of the fifth, though, with Clyde King and Clem Labine in relief, Philadelphia roared back with two runs. Phils 8, Dodgers 5.

It was a little before 4 P.M. when I looked up at the scoreboard and saw that the Giants had beaten the Braves. That meant they could do no worse than tie for the pennant. That meant we had to win this game or our year would end in utter ignominy. We needed a miracle.

Could I ask God to put on a Dodger cap?

Believe me, I thought about it.

We went down 1–2–3 in the sixth. Oisk, in relief, kept them from scoring in their half of the inning.

In the seventh, we went in order.

Top of the eighth, still 8–5. We had six outs to score three runs or the shameful catastrophe was upon us.

Pafko grounded out. We were down to five.

But just as it looked like the sun had set on our fortunes, the sun rose. Hodges singled. Cox singled. Rube Walker, hitting for Oisk, doubled them in. Phils 8, Dodgers 7. Determined to be our spoilers, the Phils didn't mess around; they brought in their ace, Robin Roberts, a 22-game winner, to end the rally. Facing Furillo, Roberts looked in for the sign. Carl got ahold of a curve and whacked it to left field. A single! Walker scored! We had caught them! We had tied the game!

Charlie turned to Big Newk. He had to contain the Phils. And in the eighth, he did just that. Mowed 'em down 1–2–3.

In the ninth, we wasted Duke's single and didn't score.

In the Philly half of the inning, Don set 'em down again.

We went to extra innings. The faint of heart had to turn away from the playing field or turn off their radios.

In the 10th, Gil singled again, but was doubled up on Cox's bunt. We didn't score.

In Philadelphia's half of the 10th, Newk gave us a scare by hitting Eddie Pellagrini. But Eddie was stranded on first and we were into the 11th inning.

Reese singled, but that was it. We didn't score.

Another 1–2–3 inning for Newk.

Top of the 12th. No nails left to bite.

We went down in order.

Bottom of the 12th. Newk walked Robin Roberts. Pellagrini bunted safely. Two on, no out. Ashburn forced Pellagrini at second, Roberts went to third. First and third, one out.

Newk walked Willie Jones intentionally.

Bases loaded, one out.

The tension was crazy.

A long sac fly would end our season.

Del Ennis at the plate. With every pitch, I held my breath. When Ennis looked at strike three, I exhaled.

Bases loaded, two out.

Newk was almost out of the inning. He just had to get Eddie Waitkus. But when Waitkus belted a line drive to the right side of the infield, my heart sank. We had lost the pennant. It was over. Except . . . it wasn't!

Jackie made an impossibly long lunge and it looked like . . . yes, he speared the ball! In doing so, he jammed his elbow into his stomach with such force that he lost consciousness. All the while, though, the ball stayed in his glove, Waitkus was out, and we were out of the inning. Jackie came to, shook it off, and ran to the dugout as if he'd just executed a routine play.

We had dodged several bullets. It was 8–8 going into the 13th.

How much more could anyone stand?

We did nothing in the 13th.

In the bottom of the inning, Don got the first two hitters, but walked Seminick and Roberts again. Dressen yanked Don for Bud Podbielan, who got the third out. On to the 14th.

We were standing at the top of the dugout. We'd been standing there for hours. We watched as Pee Wee popped out, then Duke popped out, then Jackie got ahold of one. The crack of the bat made that sound, that beautiful, satisfying, sensational sound that said cowhide had kissed wood, and the ball took off, the ball sailed, the ball soared into space—up, up into the left-field seats. It was gone! Jackie put us ahead 9–8. Campy then doubled, but Pafko grounded out to end the inning.

Bottom of the 14th. Could we hold the lead to force the Giants into a playoff?

Richie Ashburn was a great hitter. He opened up the inning with a single. Tying run on base. Winning run at the plate. Willie Jones sacrificed Ashburn to second. Tying run in scoring position. Two outs to go. We held our breath.

Del Ennis popped out.

One out to go.

It was all up to Eddie Waitkus. You could see in his eyes how badly he wanted to knock Ashburn home. He got ahold of a fast-ball, but he didn't get all of it. Pafko was under it. Pafko made the catch!

We were jumping for joy! We were celebrating like we'd won the Series—and yet what we'd really done in this miraculous game is to come back and tie the Giants as, even more miraculously, the Giants had come back to tie us.

Miracles aside, there was now no distance between us and the Giants.

There was no rest for the warriors.

No time to regroup, no reprieve.

All this happened on Sunday.

The playoff began on Monday.

In the Year of Our Lord Nineteen-Hundred Fifty-one, the Month of October

October 1

Sometimes silly little items in the morning paper caught my attention. I read the article and it stuck in my mind. Don't ask me why. There were a million more important things happening in the world—like an upcoming wedding with 600 guests, not to mention an earth-shattering climax to the most thrilling pennant contest of all time, a three-game playoff series that started in a few hours.

I'd gotten in late the night before from Philly and was enjoying my orange juice in Mount Vernon while Mom was putting breakfast on the table. Soon I'd be off to Ebbets Field, where I'd been designated to start the first game of the best-of-three playoff series. As I bit into my scrambled eggs, I started reading about a new TV show due to air in a couple of weeks. It was called *I Love Lucy* and starred Lucille Ball and Desi Arnaz. I remembered Lucy from the movies and Desi from his hit song "Babalu." At the top of my lungs, I started singing "Babalu."

Mom was startled. "Are you okay, Ralphie? What are you singing about?"

"Just loosening up the voice before I start loosening up my
arm."

Mom knew that singing always relaxed me, so she smiled as I
belted out a stirring version of "Babalu."

I called Ann.

"How are you feeling?" she asked.

"I'm singing."

"Good," she said. "When you sing, you're happy."

"Just trying to relax and not think too much."

"What were you singing?"

I started singing "Babalu" for Ann. She laughed.

"Why 'Babalu'?" she asked.

"It's Desi Arnaz's song. He's making a TV show about his wife
called *I Love Lucy*. My show is going to be called *I Love Ann*."

"Your show should be called *I'm Beating the Giants Today*. See
you at the ballpark."

In 1946, I had pitched the first game of the first play-off in history
and got beaten. That was in St. Louis. Durocher was our manager,
and Dressen was one of his coaches. Charlie had watched Leo win
the coin toss and decide to play the opening game in Missouri and
the last two in Brooklyn. That's called home field advantage. But
we lost the second game at Ebbets Field, and the Cards won the
pennant.

In 1951, Dressen, now in charge, won the coin toss. Still
determined to defy Leo's every move and make his own mark, he
decided that we should open at Ebbets Field and then move to
the Polo Grounds for game two and, if necessary, game three. The
decision mystified us.

"It's wrongheaded," said Gil Hodges, a super-shrewd baseball strategist who would wind up managing the Mets. "Why should they have home field advantage? Why should we give them the chance of playing two at the Polo Grounds?"

"Did you mention that to Charlie?" I asked.

"What good would it do? Charlie only listens to Charlie."

As I took my warm-up pitches at Ebbets Field, I was grateful to be in Brooklyn. And looking over at the boxes where I saw my entire family as well as Ann's, I was happy inside. I was relaxed, feeling strong, geared up, and ready to go.

My rhythms were right, my pitches had movement, and in the top of the first the Giants went down in order.

I also got them 1-2-3 in the second.

In our half of the inning, Pafko hit one out and the place exploded.

Dodgers 1, Giants zip.

No more scoring till the fourth, when a curveball got away from me and hit Alvin Dark. Thomson up next. Thomson hit a high, tight fastball to left field. As it went up I said to myself, "That's an out!" Then I saw Pafko start to back up and I went, "Oh, no!" He backed up 20 feet and the ball just cleared the fence at the 351-foot sign.

Giants 2, Dodgers 1.

Our bats went silent. The Giants were scoreless in the fifth, sixth, and seventh innings, but in the eighth Monte Irvin tagged me for a home run.

Giants 3, Dodgers 1.

In our half of the eighth, I was lifted for a pinch hitter. We failed to score, and failed again in the ninth.

The Giants won the opener. Larry Jansen, who pitched a fine five-hitter, got the victory. Giving up three runs and five hits, I took the loss.

It was on to the Polo Grounds, where we now had to win two straight.

October 2

I was only 25, but when I walked into the Polo Grounds on Tuesday morning, I felt like I'd been going to that park for 100 years. I thought of all the Giant games—baseball and football—that I saw as a kid. I thought of all the times I'd pitched there since becoming a Dodger. I also thought of the hurler Dressen had announced as the starter, Clem Labine, and I was glad.

Since pitching to Willie Jones from the stretch, Clem had languished in Charlie's doghouse. Apparently Dressen had finally put aside his personal grudge and decided to start him. Thank God.

Clem was sensational. He pitched a six-hit shutout. The only extra-base blow was a double by Bobby Thomson. Meanwhile, our hitters feasted on the Giant pitchers. Jackie went three for five; Duke was two for four; Jackie, Gil, Pafko, and Rube Walker, subbing for the injured Campy, each hit homers. It was a rout: Dodgers 10, Giants 0.

Series tied.

During the regular season, the Giants came roaring back. Then in the final game, against Philly, we came roaring back. And here in the second game of the playoff, we came roaring back again. It couldn't go any farther than this.

Tomorrow would end this epic battle once and for all.

Tomorrow was for all the marbles.

October 3

I was singing in the shower. I was singing "Oh, What a Beautiful Morning" from *Oklahoma!* I'd seen the show a couple of years back and loved it. I loved all the songs in all three acts. Now, don't get me wrong. I'm not saying that I wasn't nervous. I was. I'm not saying that I wasn't aware that this was probably the most important game in the history of the Brooklyn Dodgers *and* the New York Giants. I knew that. I also knew that Newk was pitching and that I'd be the number-one man in the bullpen in case he needed help. I hoped he wouldn't need help. I hoped we'd breeze through game three just like we breezed through game two. I hoped that all the talk about the Giants' historic comeback, once we crushed them today, would be silenced forever.

I was singing not because I was unaware of the tension coursing through. I was singing precisely *because* of the tension coursing through me. I was singing to release it. I was singing at the top of my lungs. It was a beautiful morning. It was gonna be a beautiful day. My hopes were high. My spirit was strong.

"Big Don," I greeted Newk when I arrived at the clubhouse, "how you feeling?"

"I'd be feeling better if Campy was catching."

"His thigh is still killing him?"

"It'd have to be killing him for him not to play."

"Rube is great," I said, referring to Rube Walker. "Rube will be terrific—and so will you."

Pee Wee and Jackie came over to join us.

"Anyone got butterflies?" asked Pee Wee.

"Not me," said Jackie in jest.

"Me, either," I joked. "Never been calmer in my life."

Hodges came over, put his arm around Newk's shoulder, and said, "Yesterday you were a 20-game winner. Today it's gonna be 21."

Although it didn't need to be mentioned, we were all aware that Don was starting on two days' rest. In our marathon win over Philly, he had pitched five and two-thirds grueling innings, giving up only one run. Along with Jackie's breathtaking catch, Newk had kept us in the game, setting up Jackie's 14th-inning blast.

That was Sunday. This was Wednesday. Today the weather was mild for October—70 degrees or so—more like spring than fall. Surprisingly, the game wasn't close to a sell-out. Out of 56,000 seats, 34,320 were sold, and probably half Dodger fans. I tried to tell myself it was just another game, but who was I fooling? In my gut, butterflies started fluttering. I walked out to the bullpen, some 455 feet from the center of action, where, together with every other Dodger pitcher, I'd watch the action. Every Dodger pitcher was a potential reliever today.

Finally, the Giants took the field. The crowd roared. Maglie made his way to the mound. With 23 wins, Sal possessed the best record in the majors (Bob Feller had 22). The Barber was one tough hombre.

The Barber got our leadoff man, Carl Furillo, looking at strike three. But then we got going: Pee Wee walked, Duke walked, and Jackie singled Pee Wee home. We drew first blood.

Bottom of the first: Giants went down in order. Newk was looking strong. Dodgers 1, Giants 0.

In the second, we went quietly.

In the bottom of the inning, after Irvin's ground out, Whitey Lockman singled. Bobby Thomson at the plate. He also singled but got caught trying to stretch it into a double. With Lockman at third, Mays lined out to left, and Newk was out of the inning.

Both pitchers were in the zone.

No score in the third.

No score in the fourth.

In the fifth, Thomson got ahold of a Newk curveball and smashed it to left. His second hit was good for a double. But he was stranded and we were still ahead 1–0.

Snider singled in the sixth but got caught trying to steal second.

In the Giants' half of the sixth, they went down in order.

Our lead was precarious but it was still a lead: 1–0.

For all the years I'd been coming to the Polo Grounds—as a kid, a teenager, and a pro—I'd never felt tension like this.

My tension was relieved a little when I started warming up. I knew it would take me a little while to get loose. My arm was stiff. But as I continued to throw, I went from feeling good to feeling extremely strong. I was still hoping, though, that I wouldn't be needed. But I knew that Newk was working with only two days' rest and could tire at any minute.

Then, in the seventh, our lead vanished. Irvin connected for a solid double. Lockman bunted him over to third, and Thomson's sac fly brought him home. Giant fans went nuts.

Just as we were tied at the end of the regular season, just as we were tied 1–1 in this playoff series, in this brutal final meeting with the Giants, we were all tied up again.

How much tighter could this get?

In the eighth inning, Furillo hit a shot back to Maglie on the mound. One out.

Then Reese singled.

Then Duke singled Pee Wee to third.

The Barber faced Jackie. His pitch was wild! Pee Wee scored, and Duke slid safely into third.

We were ahead 2–1 with a runner on third and only one out.

The Barber decided he wanted no piece of Jackie and walked him intentionally. Men on first and third.

Pafko singled off Bobby Thomson's glove at third! Duke scored! Jackie took second! 3–1!

Hodges popped out.

Billy Cox at the plate. He got ahold of Sal's curve and drove it into left field for a base hit! Jackie scored! Pafko was safe at second! We had broken it open! We were jumping up and down in the bullpen! We could smell victory!

Rube Walker grounded out to end the inning, stranding two, but the damage had been done. Our 4–1 lead was solid, especially the way Don had been pitching.

In the eighth, Don mowed 'em down 1-2-3. He was working on a four-hitter. Three more outs and, once and for all, we would have snuffed out the Giants' fire.

Larry Jansen replaced Maglie in the ninth. As expected, Dressen didn't pinch-hit for Newk, who grounded out. Furillo and Pee Wee went down.

Bottom of the ninth.

Dodgers 4, Giants 1.

We were three outs away from ending the agony.

Just three outs.

As the Giants' ninth began, I kept firing in the bullpen. Oisk was throwing and so was Labine, who had pitched a complete game the day before. Dressen wanted all options open.

I was throwing hard but thinking only one thing:

Get 'em out, Newk. Only three more, baby. Get 'em out.

As I was concentrating on my warm-up, I heard the roar of the crowd.

Alvin Dark had singled.

I threw a little harder. Another roar. I turned and saw that Don Mueller had singled to right, off Hodges' glove, sending Dark to third. Erskine and Labine, who were in the bullpen with me and saw the play, said, "Why was Gil holding Dark at first? Dark wasn't going anywhere. Not with them three runs down. The whole right side was open. Should have been a double play." Lockman then doubled, scoring Dark and sending Mueller to third, where he fractured his ankle sliding into the bag. He had to be carried off the field and was replaced with pinch runner Clint Hartung. Suddenly it was Dodgers 4, Giants 2.

Two on, no out. Tying run at the plate.

I threw harder—and so did Oisk. Newk might be tiring. We might be needed.

Irvin popped out. One gone, two to go. If Hodges had been positioned correctly, we would have been out of the inning, but we weren't.

I took a deep breath and kept on throwing.

Now it was Bobby Thomson coming to the plate, representing the winning run.

Now it was Dressen coming to the mound.

Now it was Dressen signaling to the bullpen.

Newk was out and I was in.

Now it was me making that long, long trek from the bullpen.

Later I'd hear that Sukeforth saw Oisk bounce a curveball and hesitated to use him in relief. But my guess was that, given the fact that I had far more relief innings under my belt than Carl, I'd be first choice even if Oisk hadn't thrown a pitch on the ground.

That walk from the Polo Grounds bullpen was the longest in the world, but my pace stayed steady.

I passed by Pafko, who said, "Go get 'em, Ralphie."

I entered the infield and passed by Jackie, who said, "Let's get 'em, Ralph."

I passed by Reese, who said, "No butterflies, Ralph. You're gonna get 'em."

As Newk left the mound, I told him, "Don't worry, big fella. I'll get them for you."

Dressen handed me the ball. For a second I wondered if he was going to tell me to walk Bobby Thomson to get to Willie Mays. I'd had good luck with Mays. But all Charlie said was, "Get him out." That figured. You don't put the winning run on base.

Thomson represented the winning run at the plate.

I was facing Bobby Thomson, more determined than at any moment in my life, and prepared to pitch.

I inhaled.

I exhaled.

I checked the runners, Lockman at second, Hartung at third.

I looked in for the sign.

Fastball.

I delivered a fastball directly over the plate. It couldn't have been any more down the middle.

Thomson looked at it.

Strike one!

The Giants' bench started screaming at Thomson for letting the pitch go by. They rode him hard.

"What the hell is wrong with you?" I heard Leo screaming at Bobby.

I got away with one. I couldn't get away with another.

I inhaled.

I exhaled.

I checked the runners, Lockman at second, Hartung at third.

I looked for the sign.

Fastball.

I threw it high and inside.

Thomson was waiting for it. Thomson attacked it with an uppercut swing, connected, and drove it to left field.

I turned and followed the ball's trajectory. I thought it was going to sink. It had to sink.

"Sink, sink, sink!"

I watched Andy Pafko running back to the wall . . .

"Sink, sink!"

But the ball stayed up and cleared the wall by about six inches, landing in the left-field seats.

I wanted to say it was a cheap Polo Grounds home run. I wanted to say that in any other ballpark it'd be an easy out. I wanted to believe that I was dreaming. I didn't want to believe that it was really happening. I wanted the pitch back.

But the ball was gone and the game was over. The series was over. The pennant was lost.

There was pandemonium. There was hysteria. There was Thomson rounding the bases. There was Durocher jumping up and down from the third-base coach's box like a crazy child. There was confetti flying.

After the ball sailed into the seats, I'd inadvertently picked up the rosin bag and threw it down in disgust. Head down, I headed for the center-field clubhouse.

Jackie had the presence of mind to make sure Thomson touched every base.

He did.

We were defeated.

Undone.

The White Handkerchief

NEARLY SIXTY YEARS later, I was in Los Angeles visiting my pal Vin Scully when, for the first time, he told me this story.

"Of course I was at the game," he said, "but as the junior member of the broadcast staff I wasn't announcing. Red Barber and Connie Desmond were. With microphones in front of them, they were seated in wooden chairs. I was standing. The roof of the press box was low, and even though I'm not tall, I had to bend over. When the ball was hit and Thomson started running around the bases, when all hell broke loose, I instinctively thought about Ann. I knew she was seated directly beneath me. I looked down and saw her. I can still see her now. With great dignity, she slowly opened her purse, reached in, and took out a white handkerchief. Then she closed the purse and placed it on her lap. She opened the handkerchief and placed it over her face for a very few seconds. Those few seconds said everything."

In the moments after the shock of absolute defeat, I was inconsolable. We had the game cinched and I blew it. I couldn't forgive myself. I would never forgive myself. Barney Stein caught me in what have become famous photographs. My head down, I was hiding my face in shame. I didn't want to see or be seen by anyone. Our clubhouse was dead silent. Sensing my misery, my teammates thought it best to leave me alone. What could they say? We were all shell-shocked. Only my dear friend Jackie, who knew me so well, came over and put his arm around my shoulder.

"Ralph," he said, "try not to take it personally. If it weren't for you, we would have never made it this far."

He put out his hand for me to shake. I grasped it, thanked him, and sat there for another long while. I wanted to die.

After I finally found the energy to shower and change, I left the ballpark. Ann was waiting for me, along with Father Pat Rowley, her dad's cousin and the dean of campus ministries at Fordham.

He tried to comfort me. "You did your best, Ralph."

"I blew it, Father."

"It was only one pitch. Anyone could have thrown it."

"But why me, Father?"

"At the moment when they needed their best pitcher, you got the call. That alone is a sign of the respect you have."

"*Had*," I corrected him.

"You're being too hard on yourself, son."

"But why me, Father? I love this game so much. Why did it have to be me?"

"Simple," he said. "God chose you because He knew you'd be strong enough to bear this cross. This will not weaken your faith in God, it will build the strength of your spirit."

I knew that this was Jesuit philosophy. I wanted to believe the good father's words. Part of me did believe him. Another part of me just wanted to go home and cry. But earlier that day I had promised catcher Rube Walker, my battery mate that day, that Ann and I would join him and his wife, Millie, for dinner after the game. I didn't really want to go, but I'd made the commitment and kept the date. We went to Paul Daube's restaurant, a neighborhood steak house, not far from the Polo Grounds on Courtland Avenue. When we walked in and the diners saw me, they got up and applauded.

"See that," said Ann. "You're still appreciated."

"They're Giant fans," I said. "If I were a Giant fan, I'd be applauding me, too."

After dinner, I took Ann home to Brooklyn before going back to Mount Vernon. I learned that my family had been getting hate calls. One man told my mom, "Why couldn't anyone teach your sorry son to pitch?" Most of the other callers just said, "Drop dead, Branca." My parents and siblings said to ignore the taunts. I knew they were coming from small-minded people, but the words still stung. I kept reliving that pitch. I kept thinking what if I had done this or done that. I wanted to take the phone receiver off the hook and stay inside for at least a week. I wanted to hide.

"You can't hide," said Ann when I called her before going to sleep. "Hiding is the worst thing you can do. Besides, our wedding is just a couple of weeks away, and you certainly won't be able to hide then. I think we should go to the Series game tomorrow."

"The World Series?"

"Do you know of another series?"

"Why would I want to go to the World Series?"

"To show the world you're not hiding. To show the world you have nothing to be ashamed of. You're 25 years old and you've won 76 games."

"You know my stats better than I do."

"No one knows your stats better than you, Ralph."

"I don't think it's a good idea."

"I do. It'll do you a world of good. Besides, I want to see the Yankees destroy the Giants."

"I'll think about it."

By the time I went to bed that night, I thought that Ann was right. She usually is.

In the morning, I looked at the *New York Times*. Of course it was page one news. One headline read, IT'S LIKE A WAKE IN BROOKLYN. The *Daily News* ran a screamer, THE SHOT HEARD 'ROUND THE BASEBALL WORLD. Another hit me even harder: THOMSON THE HERO, BRANCA THE GOAT. I sighed and put down the papers. The phone was ringing. When I answered it, someone yelled in my ear, "Ya, bum, ya!" and clicked off.

I got up and went to the game. I was still down, but I was determined not to let it get the best of me. I had my loving parents, my great brothers and sisters. I had my beautiful wife-to-be. I had my life. It might be a fight to pick myself back up, but I was a fighter.

Along with her parents, Ann met me at the Stadium. She looked radiant.

"Put a smile on your face," she said.

"Even if it's fake?" I asked.

"Even if it's fake," she answered.

It was fake, until a photographer spotted me and had me go over to pose with Bobby Thomson.

Understandably Bobby was all smiles.

"You want to shake his hand, Ralph?" asked Herbie Scharfman, the photographer.

"I'd rather choke him," I said, half-jokingly.

"Then go ahead," the photographer urged. "It'll make a great picture."

That was the picture that came out in the paper. Me choking Thomson, smile plastered across my face. The whole thing did not make me happy. And I was also not especially happy when the Giants, capitalizing on their momentum from their monumental victory, won game one 5–1.

Five days later, Ann and I decided to go back to the Stadium for game six. By then the Yankees had won three and were leading the Series 3–2.

In the top of the ninth, the Giants were losing 4–1 and on the verge of elimination. Exactly a week ago, they'd also been on the verge of elimination and losing to us 4–1 in the ninth inning.

Could the comeback kings come back again?

The inning opened with three consecutive singles to load the bases. Then Monte Irvin sacrificed a home run. The Giants were down by two, and guess who was coming to bat? Thomson.

Another home run here and not only would he give the Giants the lead, he could also be elected governor of New York. I leaned forward in my seat. Everyone at Yankee Stadium was thinking about Thomson's homer on October 3. Everyone wanted to see if he could do it again, even me.

When he got ahold of a fastball and drove it deep into left field, you could hear a collective gasp. But Gene Woodling got to it and, even though it was a successful sac fly, the Giants didn't score again and the Yankees won the Series that day four games to two.

The Giants' loss helped, but I had plenty else to keep my spirits up. In a few days, I'd be marrying the girl of my dreams. The wedding was wonderful. St. Francis of Assisi church was crowded with family and friends. All in white, Ann was gorgeous. I looked pretty good myself in ascot and tails. There were 12 bridesmaids and 12 groomsmen. I consider it the happiest day of my life. We ran out into the rice and a marvelous honeymoon on Sea Island, Georgia.

The honeymoon was a little bit of heaven. It was not only a beautiful spot for relaxing, but also no one bothered me about baseball. If other guests at the resort knew who I was, they acted like they didn't. And that was fine with me. I was delighted to shut out the world and simply be with Ann.

When we got back in November we moved to a little apartment in Colonial Village in Mount Vernon, where rent was $87.50 a month. Ann was happy to move close to my family and live in the city of my childhood. The insults kept coming, but there was nothing to do. I found comfort in going over some of the 1951 stats of my teammates. Campy—with 33 homers, 108 RBIs, and a .325 average—was voted MVP. Jackie hit .338. Hodges had 40 home runs and Duke 29.

I figured that eventually talk of October 3 would diminish. I figured wrong. Someone said the rosin bag I threw down after the pitch was going to the Hall of Fame in Cooperstown. A producer put out a record of Giants announcer Russ Hodges' now famous call after Thomson's homer: "The Giants win the pennant! The Giants win the pennant! The Giants win the pennant! The Giants win the pennant!" Every time I turned on the radio it seemed like that was all I heard. I did well not to throw the damn radio through the window.

My brothers were even more upset by the aftermath of the game than I was. If we were out and a stranger approached me, saying, "Hey, you're the guy who gave up the gopher ball to Thomson, ain't you?" one of my siblings would come back with, "No, that's the guy whose ERA was 3.26 last year—better than Newcombe's."

I worked in the off-season. I taught pitching at Phil Rizzuto's American Baseball Academy at an armory in upper Manhattan. My infamy also landed me a part-time job selling suits, along with Rizzuto, Yogi Berra, and Gene Hermanski at the American Shops on Broad Street in downtown Newark. I liked selling, and I liked meeting the public, but, as you'd expect, most of my customers wanted to know about The Pitch. I quickly developed a stock reply that I meant to be self-deprecating, its irony lost to me at the time: "Looked like he was waiting for it, didn't it?" I'd ask.

During the winter, when the Baseball Writers Association of America asked me to come to their dinner and do shtick with Thomson, I was hesitant—until I heard it involved singing.

"You sing in the shower," Ann liked to say, "as though you're performing for an audience of thousands. I can't ever see you turning down a chance to sing."

Thomson had been telling the press that he thought they'd been too hard on me, arguing that anyone could have thrown that pitch. I appreciated his coming to my defense and got up and did a duet, a parody of "Because of You."

In an off-key voice, Bobby sang:

Because of you, there's a song in my heart
Because of you, my technique is an art
Because of you, a fastball high
Became a dinky, chinky fly
Now Leo and me won't part
My fame is sure, thanks to your Sunday pitch
Up high and low, I don't know which is which
But come next spring, keep throwing me that thing
And I will swing, because of you

Then I took over, belting it out with all I had—and in key, mind you:

Because of you, I should have never been born
Because of you, Dodger fans are forlorn
Because of you, they yell "Drop dead!"
Several million want my head
To sever forever in scorn
One lonely bird had a word for my ear
The only girl—what a pearl—of good cheer
I lost the game but wound up with the dame
She took my name . . . in spite of you

We got a standing ovation.

"Thanks," I said, "but I just want to apologize to my wife, Ann, for the use of the word 'dame.' I meant no disrespect. I just needed a rhyme." When I sang the same words on Ed Sullivan's *Toast of the Town* show, I asked Ed to express my regrets to the TV audience for the use of the word "dame"—and he was gentleman enough to do so. He was also generous in praising my voice.

I guess I felt a little like Pagliacci, laughing on the outside but crying on the inside. At home at night, I still had nightmares about that goddamn pitch. I couldn't wait for spring training.

The Coca-Cola Catastrophe

WHEN I WENT to Vero Beach I knew Ann was pregnant with our first child—and we were thrilled. I wasn't thrilled when Harold Parrott, our traveling secretary, took away my number 13 uniform and gave me number 12 instead. Maybe he thought he was doing me a favor, but he wasn't. No matter what, I liked number 13. I didn't believe in superstitions. I didn't want to give in to triskaidekaphobia. When other guys jumped over the foul line, I stepped right on it. In my mind, it wasn't bad luck that cost us the pennant. It was a fastball high and inside.

I'd never get to wear number 13 again.

I was especially motivated that winter in Florida. I wanted to show the world that I was someone besides the guy who threw The Pitch. I felt better than I had in '51 and saw no reason why I couldn't win 20-plus again. I had 10 more good years ahead of me. Reporters were writing that no matter what I did, I'd only be remembered as the guy from October 3, but I knew if I had a series of successful seasons, I could change the story. I'd be the guy who came back from ignominy, the guy who turned the tables on the taunters.

And then came bad luck. Maybe it was brought on by that number 12 on my back.

I had just finished off a Coke when Pee Wee walked into the lobby of the navy barracks where we were staying. Rather than put the bottle on the floor, where someone might kick it over, I placed it under the chair where I'd been sitting. I got up to greet Reese. I asked him about his winter and he asked about mine.

"You aren't letting those writers get to you, are you?" he asked.

"Trying not to, Pee Wee," I said.

"Those guys got nothing better to do than criticize and second-guess. You can't let 'em drive you crazy. You gotta concentrate on something else."

"I've been concentrating on staying in shape."

"You look good, Ralph. I'm sure you're gonna have a great year."

"Thanks, Pee Wee."

Encouraged by our little talk, I went back to sit down on the metal folding chair and forgot about the Coke bottle. When my big butt hit the seat, the chair slid out from under me and I landed right on top of the Coke bottle. The bottle didn't break, but I took a direct hit just to the left of the coccyx, the bone at the base of the spine. The funny part was that I had no pain, but when I went to change for bed the blood had coagulated on my shorts.

Next morning I went to see our trainer, Doc Wendler.

"I'm looking at a severe cut shaped like a crescent," he said. "It's about half an inch deep. Eventually it'll heal and you'll be fine."

He didn't check my alignment. Months later, when I hadn't healed, I went to an osteopath. It didn't take this guy more than a minute to see what was wrong.

"You're swaybacked," he said.

"You sure?"

"Positive."

A thorough examination showed that my left side was an inch and a half higher than my right. My left side was bunched up and my right side elongated. In short, I was seriously out of alignment.

"What can I do about it?"

"Not much, I'm afraid. I'll put you back in alignment, but you'll probably not stay that way because you have been out of alignment so long." He proved to be right, unfortunately.

"Will it affect my pitching?"

"I'm sure it already has."

"Will it ever improve?"

"Probably not. But it's difficult to speculate. You'll just have to see."

Pitchers are strange animals. Even though the act of pitching— exerting the muscles in your arm to an unnatural, extreme, and dangerous degree—is perhaps the most injury-prone in sports, we think we can go on forever. We want to go on forever. We're a determined species. We think that no matter the pain, we can pitch through it. We don't want to accept the fact that an injury can permanently take us down. At least that was my attitude.

Of course, things changed in 1974, when a doctor replaced a ligament in Tommy John's elbow with a tendon from his forearm. That extended his career 13 more years. He wound up winning 164 more games, only one less than Sandy Koufax won during the span of his entire career. Tommy John surgery would be a blessing for many pitchers.

In the early fifties, though, arm and back injuries were understood far less than they are today. Basically, the expectation was to *man up and tough it out*. That's the attitude I adopted. Even when told the severity of my misalignment, I was determined that it would not hold me back.

It did. I struggled through another five years of pitching, but I was never the same. There were some days when I had good stuff, but there were more times when I had to get by with guile and control. The plain truth is that the fall to the floor in Vero Beach during spring training was career-shattering. I didn't see it then, but I do now. In retrospect, six decades after the fact, it's clear that for all my denials at the time, my pitching was permanently compromised.

In '52, however, the Dodgers were not compromised by the disaster of '51. The Dodgers roared back and beat the Giants by four and a half games to win the pennant.

Newk was not with the team that year, doing his military service. I tried to enlist again, eager to do my part in the Korean War, but, as before, a punctured eardrum and asthma kept me out.

Rookie Joe Black took up where Newk left off. Joe was a terrific addition, leading the pitching staff with a 15–4 record. I was amazed by Joe's success, because in my mind he did not have the overpowering stuff to be that effective. It was an aberration. After that he won only 14 more games in the big leagues. Fifty-two was also the rookie year for outfielder Sandy Amoros, whose immortal star turn would come in the 1955 World Series. In 1952, hurlers Carl Erskine, Preacher Roe, Billy Loes, and Ben Wade also had fine seasons. I did not. I started only seven games, winning four and losing two. My ERA wasn't terrible, at 3.84, but I was not the same pitcher. My fastball had lost its kick, my ball movement was erratic, and my timing was off.

Comic relief helped lift my sinking mood.

During a series with the Giants, Pee Wee came to our clubhouse at the Polo Grounds with this story:

"Hey, Ralph," he said, "you know how Duke, Erskine, Walker, and I carpool from Brooklyn. Well, today I'm driving up the West Side Highway and get stopped by a cop. He tells me I was speeding. 'He was,' Duke kibitzes, 'give the bum a ticket.' I hand him my driver's license. 'Harold Henry Reese,' says the cop. 'Are you Pee Wee Reese of the Dodgers?' 'Yes sir,' I say. 'Doesn't matter,' says Duke. 'Give the bum a ticket.' 'Are you on the way to the game?'" the cop asks. 'I am, sir,' I say. 'Well, good luck, Pee Wee. Before you go, if you could give me an autograph, that'd be great.'

'Are you asking me to sign the ticket?' I ask. 'No, there's no ticket. Just sign my Dodger schedule. I keep it on me at all times.'"

"Great story, Pee Wee," I said.

The next day Pee Wee arrived at the Polo Grounds with Duke by his side.

"Okay, Duke," said Pee Wee, "tell Ralph what happened today."

"It was my turn to drive," Duke explained. "We're going up the West Side Highway again when wouldn't you know it—I get pulled over. Different cop than yesterday. Says I was speeding. Wants to see my license. 'Give him a ticket, Officer,' says Pee Wee. Cop looks at my license. 'Edwin Donald Snider,' he says. I say, 'Actually, I'm known as Duke Snider. I play for the Brooklyn Dodgers.' 'Give him a ticket,' Pee Wee keeps saying. 'I'm the center fielder,' I say, 'and if you'd like an autograph, I'd be happy to give you one.' 'I sure as hell would like an autograph,' says the cop. 'Sign this ticket. I'm a Giant fan. I hope they hand you your ass today.'"

Humor aside, it was a rough year for me. After July, I didn't win another game. My arm turned stiff as a board and I was placed on the 30-day disabled list. The rest did me good. When I came back, I came back strong, giving up only one run in six innings. We had a lock on the pennant and, while I had no illusions of starting a World Series game, I felt sure I could contribute as a reliever. But Dressen wasn't going to allow that. When Dressen saw me, he saw nothing but The Pitch. I represented the nightmare season when Leo made a fool of him. So I wasn't totally surprised when Charlie waited till after the World Series eligibility deadline to reinstate me on the roster.

I watched the Series from the dugout. It was a helluva battle. Duke hit .345 with 10 RBIs and eight homers. Pee Wee hit safely 10 times for a .345 average. But alas, another Yankee-Dodger nail-biter ended in our defeat. In game seven, at Ebbets Field, Allie

Reynolds beat Joe Black 4–2. The difference was two Mickey Mantle home runs and Billy Martin's amazing infield catch in the seventh inning with the bases loaded. It was the fourth consecutive world championship for the Yanks, matching their streak from '36 through '39.

That year, the pain of another Series defeat was assuaged by the birth of our beautiful daughter Patti. My $4,200 World Series check came in handy when it came to paying doctors and buying diapers. Eleven months later an equally beautiful daughter named Mary would be born. Our little family was complete. No father has ever been prouder, and no mother more loving and attentive than Ann.

Come 1953, I was still determined to pitch through my physical problems. My arm was sore, but I told myself that with careful and conscientious training I'd be back in form.

In 1953, I was not back in form. That incontrovertible fact was hard to take. But far more devastating was another fact I learned that year—one that sent my mind reeling and my heart aching for years to come. Even now I find it hard to get my head around this inconceivable fact.

One Wollensak Telescope

THE DODGERS KEPT getting better. In 1953, a happy-go-lucky switch hitter named Junior Gilliam joined the squad that would win 105 games to claim the pennant 13½ games in front of the Braves, who had moved to Milwaukee. (The Giants placed fifth, 35 games behind.) That was the year Furillo led the league with a .344 average; Duke hit .336 and blasted 42 home runs; Jackie hit .329, and Campy stroked 41 homers and led the league with 142 RBIs.

On one hand, I was proud and excited by the greatness of our team; but on the other, I was crestfallen over my inability to convince Dressen that I could still pitch effectively. He used me only in relief during games where we were getting hammered. When I complained, Charlie placed me on waivers. No National League team picked me up, and subsequently the Dodgers let me go. My contract was for $15,000. Now that I was available to the American League, Detroit expressed interest. Just before the midseason All-Star break, I became a Tiger.

Saying good-bye to my Brooklyn brothers wasn't easy. It wasn't easy for Ann, either. She had grown close to the wives. The family feeling in Brooklyn was real; the bond was strong.

"We're rooting for you, Ralphie," said Preacher. "We're all counting on you to make a big comeback in Detroit."

"Hutch believes in you," said Oisk, referring to Tiger manager Fred Hutchinson. "He was a pitcher himself. He knows you got what it takes."

"Hey, big guy," said Newk, "just want to thank you for standing with me in St. Louis."

He was referring to the fact that at the Chase Hotel, African Americans couldn't use the pool or restaurants. They'd have to eat in their rooms. "I can fight for my country," said Newk, just back from the service, "but I can't eat in the dining room with white people. That's some bullshit." Along with Jackie, Campy, Joe Black, Duke, Pee Wee, Gil, and the other Dodgers, we made such a stink that the hotel changed its policy.

"Gonna miss you, Ralph," said Hodges, "but maybe this change is what you need."

"I'm just glad I don't have to hit against you," said Duke.

"You give 'em hell over in that American League," urged Campy. "I'll be watching you. I'm rooting for you."

There was so much good feeling—so much soulful camaraderie—among the Dodgers that leaving that team was one of the toughest emotional moments of my life. I was leaving home.

We rented our new home in Detroit from Mr. Hockey, Gordie Howe. Ann, our two infant girls, and I settled down to a new life.

Detroit was not a contender. Where the Dodgers looked for ways to win, the Tigers looked for ways to lose. I threw a couple of good games in September and my ERA, 4.15, was the best among Detroit pitchers, but I wound up the season a lackluster 4–7. The misalignment was still playing tricks on me. My arm was still sore, but I wasn't about to say anything to anyone. I wanted to keep pitching.

The Tigers wound up the '53 season 40½ games behind the Yankees, who faced the Dodgers. This was the fifth subway Series in seven seasons. In those years New York City dominated the game in a way that had never happened before and has never happened since.

Ann and I went to the Series. It was strange to watch my team from the stands. But along with all the diehard Brooklyn fans, I cheered my old teammates. Given the power of the Dodger lineup and the excellence of the pitching staff, this had to be the year to break the drought and win the first world championship.

It didn't happen. The Whitey Ford-Billy Martin-Mickey Mantle-Yogi Berra-Gene Woodling-Gil McDougald-Allie Reynolds-Phil Rizzuto Yankees won in six games, making it five straight world championships for the Bronx Bombers. *Five.* In the opinion of this old-timer, that record will never be broken.

Oisk had a beautiful game three, when he struck out 14, including four strikeouts of Mantle. But the Yankees were too much. Yogi hit .429 and Martin .500, including 12 hits and the game-winning run in the Series-winning game six. In 20 World Series attempts, the Yankees had now won 16. In seven World Series tries, the Dodgers had lost all seven. Wait till next year.

The next year in Detroit, I became good friends with my Tiger teammate Ted Gray, a great guy. He was number 34, and I was 35. Our lockers were next to each other, and we roomed together on the road. Ted was a left-handed thrower also in the twilight of his career. The 1954 Tigers were going nowhere fast—we'd wind up 43 games behind the pennant-winning Indians—and the spirit of competition was all but exhausted. Ted and I spent a lot of time talking about the past. We were veterans—at 29, Ted was a year older than I was—with many stories to share.

One night we were at a hotel in Cleveland. As usual, we had dinner together. We liked to talk about our families and plans for the future. We spoke with open hearts. We kept talking as we went up to our room. Just before going to sleep, Ted turned to me and said, "Ralph, there's something I shouldn't tell you, but I feel like I must."

"What is it?" I wanted to know.

"I was sworn to secrecy. I promised not to, but when I hear you talk about '51 and that pitch to Thomson, it breaks my heart that you don't know."

"Don't know what?"

"He knew you were going to throw him a fastball."

"You mean he guessed."

"No, he *knew*. They were stealing the signs."

"Durocher is good at stealing signs. So is Dressen. Sometimes the runner at second base can steal them as well. Sometimes they get 'em right, and sometimes they don't."

"Listen to me, Ralph. I'm not talking about on-the-field sign stealing. Everyone does that. I'm talking about a World War II telescope called a Wollensak that lets you see a fly on a chimney 300 feet away. Remember Hank Schenz?"

"Sure. Reserve third baseman. The Giants picked him up from Chicago in '51."

"Well, Hank was in the navy. He's the one who had this expandable telescope. He told Herman Franks about it."

"Herman was coaching the Giants in '51."

"Right. And then Herman told Leo. Leo said, 'Wow! Let's use it!' That's how it started."

"Who told you this, Ted?" I asked.

"Earl Rapp."

"The Giants also picked him up in '51," I remembered.

"He's an old friend. We met back in Buffalo in '46. He's a straight shooter. He's telling the truth."

"But how did it all work?"

"You know the Polo Grounds better than anyone, Ralph. You know how the Giants' clubhouse sits out there in dead center field. Leo's office is right there. It looks directly into home plate. So

170

Herman would turn off the lights so no one could see him, sit in the back of Leo's office right there in the shadows, aim the telescope at the catcher, and see the signs clear as day."

"But how did they send the signs to the hitters?"

"They had buzzers."

"You're kidding."

"I wish I were. Rapp said they had secretly laid these wires from Leo's office to the bullpen and the dugout. I mean, it was a whole system. Remember I mentioned Hank Schenz?"

"Yeah. He hardly played in '51."

"That's because he was the one buzzing the buzzer. Herman had the telescope. Herman was an ex-catcher, so he knew all about signs. If, for instance, Campy changed signs in the middle of the game, Herman could pick that up right away. Once he read the sign, he'd tell Schenz to buzz Sal Yvars, the backup catcher, who'd be sitting in the bullpen. Sal would have a towel in his hand. If it was a fastball, he'd hold on to the towel. If it was a curve, he'd wave it. A changeup or slider, he'd flip the towel over his thigh."

"I can't believe it."

"I couldn't either, Ralph, but I know it's true. You see, they had it going two ways. They had Sal signaling the hitter, but they also had a buzzer that told the guys in the dugout what was coming. If the buzzer told them a fastball was coming, they'd yell to the hitter, 'Sock it!' If the buzzer said that the catcher had called for a curve, they'd holler, 'Be ready!' If it were a changeup or a slider, they'd scream out, 'Watch it!' So the hitter had two ways of knowing what to expect—one from Sal in the bullpen and another from the guys on the bench."

"When did all this start?" I asked, my mind reeling, my throat dry, my heart pounding.

"July 19. Earl said that's when they had a meeting when Leo told the team what they were going to do."

"And no one objected? Not even Al Dark? Al's a religious guy.

I know Al wouldn't want to go along with that kind of cheating."
I was also surprised that Eddie Stanky, my roommate in Brooklyn,
would go along because he was a very religious Catholic, but then
again, he was mad at the Dodgers for trading him to the Boston
Braves in 1948.

"According to Rapp, everyone went along with the plan. They
loved the plan. The plan got them to winning."

"That's when they started streaking. That's when they started
catching up with us—after this telescope business."

"That's right. You study their win-loss record. Before the telescope, they were one team. After the telescope, they became
another. The telescope got them the pennant."

"And Thomson," I said. "Thomson knew what I was going to
throw him on October 3."

"He sure as hell did. Go back and study the stats," said Ted.
"Look at how Thomson hit off you before the telescope, and then
look at how he hit afterward."

"I will." I did. He hit .256 before the sign-stealing, with zero—
yes, zero—home runs.

"You'll see. It's like night and day."

"So what you're saying is that the whole thing's a fraud. The
pennant race. The way they caught us. The way they won the
third game. The whole goddamn thing was rigged."

"It comes down to one thing, Ralph. You got cheated. They
stole the pennant."

I couldn't sleep that night. I couldn't sleep the next night. I kept
tossing and turning. After the initial shock, my first reaction was
rage. I was infuriated. How could they do that? If Dressen had told
us he was installing a sophisticated telescope and buzzer system to
steal signs, we wouldn't have stood for it. Pee Wee had too much
integrity. So did Duke. So did Gil. So did Jackie and Newk and
Campy and Oisk. We would have told Dressen to forget about it.

We would have said either we beat 'em fair and square or we don't beat 'em at all. I would quit the team rather than be complicit to an elaborate system of secret electronic sign-stealing.

I kept reviewing the '51 season. It was uncanny the way the Giants had started to streak. It did seem unnatural. And then I remembered something Carl Erskine had mentioned one day at the Polo Grounds.

"Funny," Carl said, "that when you look at the windows out there in the Giants' clubhouse, they're all lit except for one. Wonder what that's about?" That one was Durocher's office, where Herman Franks and Hank Schenz stole the signs. They also had removed the screen so they could see more clearly.

At the time, the comment seemed innocuous. I really didn't give it much thought. But now I see that we were naive.

But was there any way in the world Ted could be wrong? Could Earl Rapp have been exaggerating? I had to find out for myself, so I called Sal Yvars, the Giants' bullpen catcher in '51. Sal and I had known each other since we were kids. He'd gone to White Plains High. As teens we played each other in both baseball and basketball.

I got him on the phone. In '53 the Giants had traded him to the Cards, so I knew he had no reason to protect Durocher. I also knew Sal was a chatterbox, but a straight-up guy who didn't lie.

"Say it isn't so, Sal," I said.

"What isn't so, Ralph?"

"That you guys had a telescope and a whole buzzer system back in '51."

"Who told you that?"

"Earl Rapp told Ted Gray, and Ted told me."

"Earl should have kept his friggin' mouth shut."

"So it's true."

"Sure it's true."

"This whole business—the scope, the wiring to the dugout and the bullpen—it really happened?"

"I was there. I was part of it. I got buzzed in the bullpen."

"And you didn't feel bad about it, Sal?"

"I felt bad for you, Ralph, when Bobby hit that homer. You got a bad rap—that's for sure."

"But none of you objected to Leo?"

"Come on, Ralph. There was no arguing with Leo. Leo loved the whole thing—especially when it turned our season around. But Leo also got worried we'd get found out. So if we were ahead by five or six runs, he'd tell Al Dark or Eddie Stanky to swing and miss real bad on a curve—even if they knew the curve was coming. Then if we were ahead by seven or eight, we'd stop stealing them altogether. But if it was a close game, you better believe we'd be on every pitch."

"And the big game in '51. The October 3 game, Sal. You were stealing signs that game?"

"Are you kidding? Why wouldn't we be stealing signs on the biggest game of the year? Leo's crooked, but he's not crazy."

"And Thomson's at-bat against me. You were feeding Thomson the signs?"

"Two fastballs—I remember it like it was yesterday. Your first one was over the plate. Bobby should've swung. Then Rube gave you the sign for another fastball. I let Bobby know to expect the same. You threw it up and in, and he hammered it."

"G'damn!" I said.

"The guys will be on me for admitting this to you, Ralph, but it's the truth."

"I appreciate that, Sal, I really do."

"Look, Ralph, you're a good guy and I wish it hadn't been you who threw Bobby that pitch. I wish Dressen had brought in Erskine instead of you. Hope you don't hold it against me, Ralph, but you gotta understand—I was just the messenger. Besides, you know Leo. If he thought it meant winning a game, he'd murder his mother."

Then I asked, "Well, how did you do so well on the road?"

His answer floored me.

"We also stole them on the road."

"What? How?"

"Franks and Schenz sat in isolated seats in center field in all the away parks and gave the signs. They figured out how to camouflage what they were doing. Pittsburgh was the only one where they couldn't get close enough to center field to be 100 percent accurate. On the last day in Boston, I gave the sign out of the bullpen in right-center to Lockman. He couldn't hit Warren Spahn at all, but he knew a curve was coming and slapped a double to left field, scoring the two winning runs."

"What about Ebbets Field?" I asked Yvars. "Would they use the telescope in Ebbets Field?"

"Never. They were too scared. They knew if any of the fans caught them, they'd never get out alive."

When I got back to Detroit, I told Ann the whole story.

"That's horrible," she said. "That's simply horrible. You should file a complaint with the commissioner."

"I don't think so, honey."

"Why not?"

"I don't want to be a crybaby," I said. "I don't want to be seen as a sore loser."

"I understand, Ralph. You just want to put it behind you."

"I'd like to. I'd like to forget it ever happened."

But I couldn't. And, according to my brother John, even if I could, the world was entitled to know the truth.

John was the second person I told. John was a man of impeccable character. Later in life, he became a state legislator and New York boxing commissioner. He was a civic leader, highly respected and loved by all. And, of course, he was my biggest defender.

"This rap you've been getting, Ralph, this idea of you being the goat is all based on bullshit. You weren't the goat. You were the victim of a calculated scheme. You need to get the truth out there. You need to vindicate yourself."

"At what cost, John? I'll just look like a baby crying over spilt milk. I don't want to be the one to point the finger."

"But you've been wronged."

"A lot of people have been wronged."

"What if I go to the press?"

"Don't. No one will believe you anyway."

"You mean you're not mad about it?"

"Of course I'm mad. I'm mad as hell. The goddamn Giants took food off our table. That World Series money should have been ours, not theirs. They cheated our fans out of their bragging rights. What they did was scandalous, but I don't want to be the one who breaks the scandal. That's not me."

Of course, I was *not* able to put it behind me. On a public level, I could restrain myself—and did—from going to the press. But privately, I was haunted. I went back over the stats. The Giants won 37 of their last 44 games. Imagine how many of those games were won because their hitters knew what was coming. If their cheating had given them one single victory—and common sense says it gave them a lot more than that—then they caught us unfairly. There never should have been a playoff. We fought and won the pennant, only to get robbed.

As for Thomson, after they installed the buzzer system, his batting average went up by more than 100 points. When he wasn't getting the signs, he hammered 9 home runs; when he was, he hit 24. Three of those late-season home runs were against me. And the big one on October 3—the one that broke my heart, the hearts of my teammates, and Brooklyn fans the world over—was the homer that raised Bobby to legendary heights. There he stood, a nice man, a husband and a father, a hero. Could I be the guy who destroyed all that? The answer was no.

•

In July 1954, the Tigers released me. No surprise. Ann, the girls, and I moved to a house in White Plains. Not quite knowing what to do with myself, I started working out at the local ball field. I noticed that my arm was back. And like the never-say-die optimist that I am, I convinced myself that I could still strike out major league hitters consistently. When I saw that the Yankees were in town for a long home stand, I called Casey Stengel.

"I know you think I'm crazy, Case, but I think I still got it," I said. "I've been throwing strikes for a couple of weeks now."

"I don't think you're crazy, Ralphie. I think you're a pitcher. And pitchers always think they have another great season in them. And who knows? Maybe you do. Come down to the Stadium and pitch batting practice."

Encouraged, I showed up early.

"I'll get someone to warm you up," Casey said, pointing to Mantle.

"Catch Branca for a while, will you, Mick? And Ralph, don't hurt the kid. His hands are worth good money."

Casey liked what he saw, took me on, and gave me number 24. Suddenly I was a New York Yankee. This was the year when the Yankees, usually in first, found themselves trailing the Indians. In less than a week I effectively relieved against the White Sox in Chicago. In August, I got to start in Baltimore. The umpire squeezed me and I walked too many in four-plus innings but gave up only one run. Phil Rizzuto was playing shortstop and kept yelling at the ump, "Where are those pitches?" They were knee high and over the plate, but he was an American League umpire, and their strike zone was above the knee, not like the National League zone, which included the whole knee.

My next start for the Yankees was on August 14 against the Red Sox, also Old-Timers' Day. Vince Scully once said, "It's a mere moment in a man's life between the All-Star game and an old-timers' game." On that dog day of summer in 1954, I was closer to understanding that sentiment than I realized.

I pitched well for six innings, giving up one run. With the score tied 1–1, Bill "Moose" Skowron pinch-hit and cracked a double, scoring two, making me the winning pitcher for the last time in the major leagues.

The 1954 World Series saw the Giants sweep the Indians four straight. It was the sixth straight championship for a New York City team and remembered for one play—Willie Mays's sensational back-to-the-plate basket catch of Vic Wertz's mighty blast to deep right-center field in the Polo Grounds, a beautiful moment in the history of our beloved sport, no matter how one feels about the New York Giants and Leo Durocher.

My beloved career was winding down, but the end wasn't easy. I kept hanging on to hope. My passion for pitching was still driving me. I kept in shape in the off-season and showed up for the winter meetings that the owners and managers hold every year. In 1955, it was in New York. I wasn't proud. I wanted to pitch. When the Giants showed interest, I hesitated. This was the team, after all, that had been my undoing. At the same time, the Giants also were the team of my childhood dreams. I thought of the Giants of Mel Ott, not Leo Durocher. Besides, it meant I would be closer to home than ever. And it also would mean that I could say I'd pitched for all three New York City teams. I liked the sound of that. There was, however, one caveat. My $15,000 salary would be cut in half and I'd have to start, not with the Giants, but with their Class AAA American Association farm club, the Minneapolis Millers. This was a test of my passion for pitching. Would I humble myself?

Hell, yes. Give me the ball, coach, and let me strike out these sons of bitches!

I gave 'em hell in spring training, going 15 innings without giving up a run. I thought I was back. But in the regular AAA season I ran into problems. Of the 19 initial hits I gave up, eight were homers. The hitters were getting to me. And so were the fans.

"Hey, Branca!" one screamed. "Where's your buddy Thomson?"

"Is it true," yelled another, "that you're banned from Brooklyn for life?"

"You're a sad sack!"

"You're a has-been!"

"You're a bum!"

Finally, I turned to those jerks and let 'em have it: "What ball team have you guys ever played on? The Bloomer Girls?"

After the game, a couple of guys on the Millers tried to console me. Al Worthington and Alex Konikowski had played for the Giants.

"We heard those fans out there, Ralph," said Alex, "and they were out of line. There's something you should know about the '51 season. I don't know if what we're gonna say will make you feel better or worse."

"I know what you're gonna say," I said. "Earl Rapp and Sal Yvars explained it in detail."

"We just wanna say we're sorry," said Al.

"I appreciate it, guys, but that chapter is over. Time to turn the page."

How Sweet It Is

MINNEAPOLIS RELEASED ME in mid-July and, as a husband and dad, I was happy to be home. I was both disappointed and relieved at missing the chance to put on a New York Giants uniform.

Meanwhile, 1955 was perhaps the greatest year in the history of the Dodgers. Their World Series victory over the Yanks was the culmination of a long-held dream. It really happened. Brooklyn beat the Bronx.

Ann and I went to the games. During the regular season the Dodgers performed brilliantly, finishing 13½ games ahead of the Braves—Newk rebounded with a 20–5 year—while the Yankees barely beat out the Indians. (This also was the rookie year of Sandy Koufax, the greatest pitcher of the modern era. It'd take Koufax a few seasons, though, to find his form.)

The Yankees had taken it to the Dodgers five straight times, each loss more painful than the last. So the sweetness of this success, half a century in the making, was extreme.

Before the Series began, Dodger coach Billy Herman asked me to come by the Ebbets Field clubhouse.

"Ralphie," he said, "you got more experience than anyone on this club against the Yanks. Not only that, you've been playing with them."

"What are you saying, Billy? You want me to put on a uniform and start game one? I'm ready."

Herman laughed. "You're always ready, Ralph. But seriously, will you go over the Yankee hitters with me one by one, so I can be sure our staff knows how to pitch to them?"

"Are you kidding? Let's get started."

"Hank Bauer," said Billy.

"Hank likes the ball high. Keep it down. Curve him. Fool him with a changeup."

"Gil McDougald."

"He's tough," I said. "He hits it all over. You gotta move it around. Principally, pitch him low."

"Berra."

"You can count on Yogi going after the first ball and the fastball."

"What about Mantle?"

"Always trouble. He'll sit on the fastball. Pitch him down and away. Sometimes the changeup will fool him."

"And Moose Skowron?" asked Billy.

"High-ball hitter. Keep it down."

"This rookie—Elston Howard."

"This is a guy you wanna curve. Be careful. He's got power."

"Rizzuto."

"No power. High-ball hitter. He'll bunt on you."

"Billy Martin."

"Tough out. He likes 'em high and fast."

"Can any of the pitchers hit?" he asked.

"Whitey can hit. And Tommy Bryne is a terrific hitter. Tommy's never an easy out."

"This helps, Ralph. Thanks a lot."

"No problem, Billy. But I still think I'm your starter for game one."

•

Don't get me wrong. I'm not saying my tips resulted in us winning the Series in '55. It just felt great to contribute, even in a small way, to a team I loved.

The Dodgers beat the Yanks in '55 because, man for man, they were better. The old-timer in me also has to say that I believe the Dodgers would have beaten the Yankees in '51 for the same reason. I can be more objective about '55, though, because I wasn't on the team.

I was in the stands when, as game one began, I reviewed the situation: The Bombers hadn't lost a Series since 1942. In the past 14 years, they'd played the Dodgers in five Series and won every one. But this year, although their power was great—Mantle hit 37 homers and Yogi 27—and their pitching strong—Whitey Ford, Bob Turley, and Tommy Byrne were all double-digit winners—I didn't see them as a match for Campy (.318 and 32 homers), Duke (.309 and 42 homers), or Furillo (.314 and 26 homers).

The first two games, at the Stadium, proved me wrong. In the opener, Newk got hit hard and lost to Whitey Ford 6–5. (In that game, rookie Elston Howard's home run made the difference. Elston was the first African American to play for the Yankees—eight full years after the Dodgers signed Jackie.)

In game two, Tommy Byrne pitched a five-hit 4–2 victory. It didn't look good.

The next day, though, Johnny Podres looked really good at Ebbets Field. On his 23rd birthday, he gave Dodger fans the gift of shutting down the Yankees 8–3. We were back in it.

In game four, Brooklyn's bats caught fire. Campy hit two round-trippers and we won 8–5. Series tied.

In game five, we made a clean sweep of our home stand and won 5–3, with two homers from Duke. We were one game away from our first Series win.

Back at the Stadium, it was all Whitey Ford. He gave up only four hits and won 5–1. Series tied.

Tuesday, October 4, 1955. All-or-nothing game seven. Stadium packed. Dodger skipper Walter Alston went with Podres again. Casey tapped Tommy Byrne, winner of game two. It was a close one. The Dodgers led 2–0. In the bottom of the sixth, Sandy Amoros replaced George Shuba in left. Podres walked Billy Martin. McDougald laid down a bunt base hit, and the Yanks had two on with nobody out. Berra at the plate. First-ball-swinging Yogi cracked a line drive to left that looked like a certain double. Two runs would score to tie the game, but wait . . . Amoros reached out to make a spectacular one-handed catch on the run and somehow got the ball back to Reese, who relayed it to Gil to double McDougald off first. The rally was dead, and three innings later, thanks to Amoros and a gallant effort by young Johnny Podres, the drought had ended. Glory had arrived. Dodger fans finally didn't have to invoke the cry of "wait till next year." Next year had come. And for the seventh year in a row, a New York City team was crowned world champs.

A beautiful thing happened in 1956. I was back on the Dodgers. I had considered buying a sporting goods store in Mount Vernon, but gave up the idea when I felt my arm getting stronger. The pitcher in me was not ready to go gentle into that good night. The pitcher in me still hungered to pitch.

Sometimes I'd drive over to Ebbets Field, where I'd be asked to throw batting practice. The irony was not lost on me. I had begun in Ebbets Field throwing batting practice in 1942, when I was 16. Fourteen years later, at age 30, I was back doing the same thing. But that was all right. I'd be the last to say that humility is a quality that comes naturally to me, but at this point I had no choice. It was batting practice or nothing.

I did it for practically the entire month of August. Humility paid off. In early September, manager Walter Alston thought I was ready, and general manager Buzzy Bavasi offered me a modest contract. I grabbed it. I'd be ineligible for the World Series, but maybe

I could help the team, which was in a close three-way contest with the Braves and the Reds. Either way, it was wonderful being back with my brothers.

In my first game back with Brooklyn, on September 7, I faced—you guessed it—the Giants. I relieved for two innings, giving up a hit and no runs—plus I struck out Willie Mays and Bill Sarni. I didn't know it at the time, but when I set the Giants down in the top of the ninth and went back to the Dodger dugout, I'd never pitch in a major league game again.

I thought another chance would come later that year. When Newk and Oisk had sore arms, Jackie said, "Why isn't Alston putting you in?"

"Ask him, Jackie," I said. "He's managing."

"He's a gutless bastard."

I watched the '56 World Series from the stands. It was another subway Series—the fifth in six years—and there wouldn't be another for 46 years when, in 2000, the Yankees beat the Mets in five. The Series was an old song with only a slightly different melody. The Yanks beat us in seven. It was game five, though, that baseball fans will never forget. At Yankee Stadium, Don Larsen achieved the seemingly impossible. He pitched a perfect World Series game. And, although I was rooting against him, as a pitcher, I was proud for him. A perfect game is a peerless athletic feat. Don's achievement will live forever.

I knew my arm would not hold out forever, but at 31 I wasn't prepared to face that fact. Alston put together a Dodger team that went to Japan in the winter, where I did some pitching. I was hurting, but still determined. Back in Florida for spring training, the pain was too much. Even this obstinate pigheaded pitcher called Ralph Branca had to admit that the time had come.

I'd been a good starter, a good reliever. I'd been a workhorse. I'd been unafraid to keep on keeping on. But I couldn't argue with results. I wasn't getting anyone out.

"You can play in the Pacific Coast League," Bavasi told me.

"I appreciate it, Buzzy," I said, "but I think it's best that I retire."

"You may be right, Ralph, but remember one thing—you're retiring as a Brooklyn Dodger."

The Stigma

T HE NEXT GUY who says something to you, Ralphie," said my brother John, "bust him in the chops."

"That'll look great in the papers the next day."

"Then I'll bust the bastard in the mouth for you."

"Better let it go."

"Who'd think you'd still be getting these asinine comments?"

I'd just told John about some guy on the golf course needling me about Thomson.

After my retirement from pro ball, I was sure again that The Pitch would eventually be forgotten. I was wrong again. The drama of that day and the magic of that moment had built over time—and would continue to build for the rest of my life.

I had considered the question of what to do with the rest of my life. I had thought about going back into singing, but that meant being on the road. I had a young family and didn't relish the idea of being away. There also was the prospect of coaching in the minor leagues. That, too, involved extended time out of town. I thought about a business that would keep me close to home. Sales seemed attractive. I was a people person and, as a natural-born debater, I liked proving my case. I also knew I needed to believe in what I was selling. I searched for a product that most everyone needed. That's how I landed on insurance. As a practical guy,

I also knew that my name—whether you saw me as famous or infamous—would help get my foot in the door. Cold calls are tough, but a little easier if you hear someone say, "Ralph Branca the baseball player?" Even if I heard, "Ralph Branca the guy who pitched to Thomson?" at least I had an opening.

I worked for Security Mutual in a building atop Grand Central Station in the middle of Manhattan. I took the business seriously and completed a five-year course that certified me as a chartered life underwriter. My main interests were protection insurance and estate planning. I did well.

In 1957, my first year out of baseball, the Yankees won the pennant for the eighth time in nine years. But it was Milwaukee's year. Hank Aaron hit 44 home runs during the regular season, and Lew Burdette won three of the Braves' four wins in the Series while posting an ERA of 0.67.

The fact that the Dodgers finished third was not as alarming to their fans as the persistent rumors about a move to California. Of course the rumors proved true. By '58 the Dodgers were in L.A. and the Giants in San Francisco. Ebbets Field was demolished in 1960, the Polo Grounds four years later.

These are sad facts. Millions of people, me included, were devastated. The era when New York City baseball dominated the public imagination was gone. Two teams were gone. Fans were left without a team. The sorrow was compared to a death in the family. Walter O'Malley, the mastermind of the move, was compared to Satan. He was viciously attacked as an enemy of the people, a corporate titan interested only in profit—and to hell with the good denizens of Brooklyn.

I defended O'Malley then and I defend him now. You might think that's because, as the victim of fans' wrath, I identified with him. But that's not the reason. I knew O'Malley and saw how tirelessly he worked to keep the Dodgers in Brooklyn. He didn't want to move. He had paid for plans to build a new ballpark in the Atlantic Yards at the corner of Atlantic and Flatbush avenues in Brooklyn, a hub for subways to the boroughs and trains to the Long Island suburbs. He couldn't stay in Ebbets Field because there was room for only 700 cars. Beyond the expanded parking at the new location, O'Malley understood that the real key was public transportation. He had vision. His stadium location was so perfect that, some 55 years later, it's where the $4 billion Barclay Center is being built, the new home of the Brooklyn Nets. O'Malley was ahead of his time.

Robert Moses was not. He was, of course, the master builder responsible for everything from the West Side Highway to the Triborough Bridge to the Brooklyn-Queens Expressway. His vision of the future was to accommodate cars. His power was tremendous, exceeding the mayor's and the governor's. He once held 12 different positions; he headed the Parks Commission, the Power Commission, the Bridge and Tunnel authority—you name it and Moses controlled it. He saw the future in cold, calculated terms— a network of expressways leading out of the city. At one point he tried to build a highway through Greenwich Village. Were it not for vociferous opposition, he would have desecrated the most charming neighborhood in all New York. He never considered the Dodgers' contribution to the culture of Brooklyn, a borough of neighborhoods. Moses had no heart for neighborhoods.

When O'Malley proposed the stadium at Atlantic Yards, Moses said no. He wanted to use that location for a massive car garage. If there was to be a new stadium, Moses wanted it in the area where Shea now sits. O'Malley pointed out that that was in Queens, not Brooklyn. Moses didn't care. When O'Malley fought for his Brooklyn location, appealing to the mayor and the governor, Moses blocked him. As a public figure, O'Malley had a degree of power. Next to Moses, though, he had none. When the city of Los Angeles offered him a financial deal he couldn't refuse, he took his team and left town. Looking back, O'Malley's move is seen as one of the shrewdest in sports history. His L.A. franchise became the gold standard for all sports.

Yet O'Malley would have stayed if Moses had yielded. Beyond that, there is another fact no one likes to remember. For all the joy the Bums had brought to Brooklyn, attendance had dwindled dramatically. The same was true of the Giants. There's no doubt that the citizens of those boroughs loved their teams, but increasingly they were content to watch on TV rather than come to games. Many of the same fans who called O'Malley a monster had themselves deserted their beloved Dodgers during their final years in Brooklyn.

The loss was tremendous, but life went on.

After retiring, my love for the game and my concern for the players' welfare were as strong as ever. That's why I decided, at Warren Spahn's behest, to get involved with BAT, the Baseball Assistance Team, formed by Peter Ueberroth. As the first president and then CEO of the organization, I served in that capacity for 17 years. It was a great honor because we did great work, helping those major and minor players who'd fallen on hard times. In past eras when baseball players were not paid the same as today's players, many of them wound up hurting for money. The pension, though very nice, was not enough if you took it out in an early year. You are able to take the pension at age 45, but the value is insignificant compared to age 65. Some of the guys wound up near-destitute. Fay Vincent, baseball commissioner at the time, got the owners to make a major contribution. When Bobby Valentine got on the board, he suggested that the then-current players also would contribute, which turned out to be correct. We found corporate sponsorship and I put together an annual dinner and sold tables to raise additional funds.

To protect the privacy of the player involved, the actual work done with the money was not publicized. A couple of players, however, went public with their stories.

My teammate Sandy Amoros, the man who played such a key role in the Dodgers' first World Series victory back in '55, was living over a garage in Miami. One of his legs had been amputated and he needed a prosthetic. We took care of that in addition to finding him an apartment, where he reunited with his daughter and put his life back on track.

Stan Williams, a former Los Angeles Dodger, called me one day and told me that one of his old teammates, Steve Dalkowski, was ready to take a dive off a high bridge. Alcoholism had him in its grip. BAT reached him, put him in recovery, and hooked him up with other veterans, like Don Newcombe, who had gone public about their battles with the bottle. A year later, Dalkowski came to our dinner and went public with his story. He had the audience in tears. He was sober, holding down a job, and told the world that it's never too late to start fresh.

It turned out that baseball's owners and players, though often on opposing sides, could stand together when it came to aiding those in need.

Beyond wanting to help the less fortunate, I've also been interested in the post-baseball life of my colleagues. I like to keep up with my teammates and former opponents.

But when I ran into Bobby Thomson on the streets of Manhattan, I felt a little strange.

Hellos and Good-byes

I T WAS IN the sixties. I left my midtown office on a summer evening to head for Grand Central. The streets were crowded with commuters, hurrying to get to their trains on time.

"Hey, Ralph, funny seeing you here. How are you?"

I looked into the eyes of Bobby Thomson.

"I'm fine, Bobby. What are you doing around here?"

"I work near here. I got a job at the West Virginia Pulp & Paper Company. I'm selling paper bags. What are you up to, Ralph?"

"Same job, different product. I'm selling insurance."

"That's great. How's the family?" he asked.

"Fine. And yours?"

"Doing well, thanks. Will you be going to the Old-Timers' Game at Shea?"

"I will. I may even pitch against you, Bobby."

"Just don't bean me, Ralph."

"Never. At least not on purpose."

We shook hands and went our separate ways.

A month or so later I was at the game and, as you might expect, they asked me to pitch to Bobby.

My first throw got away from me and hit him on the foot. It was not intentional. An intentional beanball would have hit him in the head.

Herman Franks, one of the main guys who facilitated the buzzer system, was catching. Herman was a wise guy, and I didn't like him. I should have thrown a slider and broken one of his fingers. But I didn't.

When I saw Leo at the game, I should have said something like, "Why the hell did you cheat us out of our money in '51?" But I didn't. He hardly spoke to me. What did *he* have to be mad about?

"He can't look you in the eye," Ann said afterward, "because he knows how he wronged you."

The game wasn't much fun. The fans got on me. They got their jollies screaming how I was a bum, the guy who blew the pennant. Our daughter Patti, who was ten, came to the game with us.

"Why are they saying bad things about Daddy?" she asked.

"Because they don't know any better."

Howard Cosell was a friend. In 1963 he had a radio show *Speaking of Sports*, which included a postgame analysis of how the Mets did during their spring training matches. Howard put me on the show with him. Just before we went on the air, Larry Goodman, Howard's producer and also a friend, said that the wire service was running a story about the Giants cheating in '51. It mentioned a telescope and buzzers. On the air, Howard asked whether I knew about it.

"I've heard," I said, "but I don't want to talk about it."

Howard, who never tired of discussing the Thomson home run, kept after me.

"Howard," I said, "what part of *I don't want to talk about it* don't you understand?"

The next day there were a few small articles about it. Reporters asked Thomson and Leo whether it was true. They denied the existence of a telescope or buzzers. They swore up and down that the accusations were fabrications. I still wasn't about to bust them. I still didn't think it was my place. As I expected, the public showed no interest, journalists didn't pursue it, and the story died.

I wasn't quite as popular as the Beatles in the early sixties, but I did manage another 15 minutes of fame on a TV game show called *Concentration*, hosted by Hugh Downs. Basically you had to recall what was behind a board of squares. My good memory made me money. I won 17 straight games and, at least in those days, a small fortune in prizes: a pool, diamond jewelry, and a collection of fine dinnerware. I was the most successful champ in the history of the game. It was fun, profitable, and good for my ego. As an old ham, I liked all the attention.

I also liked hosting *Branca's Bullpen*, a pregame Mets show on TV during the '64 season. It kept me connected to the game I love so much. Moreover, the exposure did not hurt my insurance business. The Mets brought me even closer to Gil Hodges, who joined the expansion team in '62 and became the Mets' manager in '68.

Gil should be remembered not only as a great player but also as an astute student and innovator of the game. It was Gil who came up with the five-man rotation. And it was also Gil who brought that beautiful Brooklyn Dodger soul to the Mets.

A season after taking over, Gilly turned the team around. He was the driving force behind the "Amazin' Mets" when they won the World Series in '69. Everywhere you looked you saw old Dodgers: my old catcher Rube Walker was his pitching coach; Joe Pignatano, another former Bum, was the bullpen coach. (Rube and Joe had been Campy's backups.) Yogi might have been a Yankee, but his personality made him more like a Dodger. Berra was coaching at first base while my friend and basketball buddy from NYU, Eddie Yost, was coaching at third.

During the regular season in 1969, I dropped by the clubhouse before the game. I had roomed with Gil when we were Dodgers, and he always extended an open-door policy to me. We liked to chat it up.

"So what do you think of this five-man rotation business, Ralph?" he asked.

"To be honest, Gilly, I don't see how it's gonna work when you only have three good pitchers." Tom Seaver, Jerry Koosman, and Gary Gentry were the hurlers.

"Rube and I look at it this way," said Gil. "Seaver averages 175 pitches a day. That's a helluva lot of pitches. I don't have to tell you that Seaver is the franchise. He's our ticket this year, and we want to make sure he's well rested. We're gambling on the fact that expanding the rotation will result in more Seaver victories."

It did. Seaver won 25 in '69, and the Amazin' Mets made Dodger fans think it was '55 all over again.

Some two and a half years later, on April 2, I was sitting at home in White Plains reading the Sunday papers. The news was all about the war in Vietnam. There was a note by my phone to call Gil in two days to wish him a happy birthday. The phone rang. It was Rube Walker.

"Ralphie," he said, "you're not going to believe this, but Gil's gone. We were all with him on the golf course. He was playing like he didn't have a care in the world. You know Gilly, always a good word for everyone. He was smiling, he was joking, and then he fell. Just like that. Heart attack, Ralphie. Massive heart attack. He's gone."

There was nothing I could say. Gilly had suffered heart problems before, but he told me that the doctors had given him the right medication and all was well. Of all the Dodgers, Hodges was the strongest. He kept himself in the best shape. He seemed the most indestructible. His only bad habit was smoking. I would say two packs a day. Managing is tough, so I assume that some days he smoked even more. I loved him with all my heart.

The funeral service was at a Catholic church in Brooklyn, the borough where Gilly and his wife, Joan, had lived for most of their lives. Driving to the church, I happened to glance out my window and saw Jackie Robinson driving alongside me. I honked and waved but he didn't turn. His hair was snow white and he was wearing thick glasses. I realized that he couldn't turn because he needed all his concentration to look straight ahead. He was struggling with vision. I parked next to him. As Jackie emerged from his car, he had trouble finding his footing on the uneven sidewalk.

After we embraced, I hooked my arm in his.

"It's the diabetes, Ralph," he told me. "It's affecting my vision."

His gait was unsteady and, as we entered the grounds of the church, I was able to catch him as he tripped on the uneven flagstone pavement.

"Just like '47, Ralph," he said, "when you tackled me before I crashed into the dugout."

I thought back to Jackie's rookie year. He was the most daring base runner in all baseball. He had eyes in the back of his head. He was the very picture of vitality. His reflexes were lightning-fast, and his timing at the plate was uncanny. In a few short years, he had become old and sick. In a few short months, I would be one of the pallbearers at his funeral.

It was too much to fathom.

Ann and I had often been invited to his home in Stamford, Connecticut, on many lovely occasions. He and his wife, Rachel, loved to support charities by giving lawn parties where jazz musicians such as Ella Fitzgerald, Duke Ellington, and Dizzy Gillespie entertained. After baseball, he became an executive at Chock Full o' Nuts and the first black vice president of an American corporation. He worked tirelessly for civil rights, saying over and over again that he wouldn't be happy until a major league team named an African American manager. That didn't happen until after Jackie was gone—in 1974, when the Indians hired Frank Robinson.

On October 12, 1972, just seven months after Gilly, Jackie died of a heart attack. He was 53. His funeral was a national event. The Rev. Jesse Jackson gave the eulogy at New York's Riverside Church. Those of us who had the privilege of playing with Jackie remembered what we had known ever since that summer, some 25 years earlier, when he'd been brought up from Montreal: no other man could have represented his people with greater dignity, stamina, and skill. He was a great athlete, that's for sure. But it was Jackie's qualities as a leader—his moral courage and unwillingness to compromise his high principles—that guarantee him an indelible chapter in the history of our country.

"I remember this one time when Jackie and I were sitting in the dugout," Campy told me when I visited him in Vero Beach during the Dodgers' spring training. "He was due up that inning. 'If no one gets on base,' he said, 'I'm bunting my way on. Then I'm gonna steal my way around the bases.' 'What makes you say that, Jackie?' I asked. 'I need the exercise,' he said. Well, don't you know that's just what he did."

The story was doubly poignant because, as he told it, Campy was sitting in a wheelchair. He'd been in that chair since January 1958 when, after closing his Harlem liquor store and driving home to Glen Cove, he slid off an icy road, hitting a telephone pole. The car flipped over. His neck was broken, and for the rest of his life Campy was paralyzed from the shoulders down. After extensive therapy, he had limited use of his hands, but he never walked again.

As with Jackie, it was another instance of adjusting to a radical change in his life. You couldn't talk with Campy without remembering his agility as a catcher, his ability to rip off the mask and chase down foul balls, to put up that big target and keep that steady crouch, to block speedsters charging in from third, waiting for the throw, daring the contact, blocking the plate, absorbing the blow, and making the tag.

Campy was glorious as a catcher but equally glorious in the second phase of his career where, from that wheelchair, he took on the role of master storyteller and principal Dodger spirit of goodwill—past, present, and future. Until his death in 1993 at 71, that spirit was alive in his heart. He was always upbeat, regaling everyone around him with stories of his days in the Negro Leagues, the big leagues, the big games against the Giants and the Yanks, the umpires who got it right, and those who got it wrong. Along with Yogi and Stengel, Campy took his place as one of the sport's finest and funniest raconteurs. He was a great player before the accident; after the accident he became an even greater man.

The man from our era who continued to haunt me, of course, was Bobby Thomson. While I had been tagged as the goat, he'd achieved status as untainted hero. As decades went by, the labels became permanent; they were seared in the public imagination. The perception was unalterable: Bobby won it; I lost it.

No reexamination of the facts was expected or even wanted. The case was closed. There was nothing to do except grin and bear it.

But then, unexpectedly, something happened that changed the chemistry between Bobby and me. Like Laurel and Hardy or Burns and Allen, we became a team and, in our way, developed an act in the field of sports merchandise. Who would have guessed?

Improbable Friendship

IN THE LATE sixties I bumped into Bobby again—this time on a plane to Toronto. He was pleasant, and I was a lot less than pleasant. In the years since 1951, my cordiality had decreased. The more I lived with the idea that the Giants had cheated, the more I kept it to myself, the more I really didn't care too much about giving Thomson a hug. I didn't avoid him, but simply shook his hand and kept going.

In the seventies, I saw him again at an Old-Timers' Game in Texas. I kept my distance. What I remember most from that day, aside from seeing old friends, was what happened when I got up to pitch. Over the loudspeaker they blasted Russ Hodges's famous call "The Giants win the pennant! The Giants win the pennant! The Giants win the pennant! The Giants win the pennant!" No one had warned me that that would happen, and I can't say I was thrilled.

Pee Wee Reese ran to me on the mound and asked, "Did they tell you they were going to do that?" "No," I replied.

"That's really bush," he said.

At another Old-Timers' Day, at Yankee Stadium, Berra broke everybody up with one of his Yogi-isms.

After the announcer said, "Now, as their names appear on the big screen, a moment of silence for all those players we lost in the last year," Yogi said, "I hope I never see my name up there."

In 2003, when Berra and I were at Larry Doby's funeral with ex-commissioner Fay Vincent, Yogi said, "If we don't go to their funerals, they won't come to ours."

In the eighties, a promoter in New Jersey asked me to come to a baseball card show at a hotel. He promised me $1,000 if I signed for a couple of hours. I had never been to one of these events. Because my insurance business had been successful, I didn't have the need. I also didn't want to be reminded, still another time, of the 1951 moment everyone would want to discuss.

Bobby had been making modest money at card shows. And when the promoter said that he wanted Bobby and me to sign at the same table, I thought, *Well, maybe it's time to let bygones be bygones.*

The show had a small stream of traffic, mainly older guys going from table to table to see what rare baseball cards were available. When the promoter took me to the ballroom, Bobby was already seated behind a table. In front of him was a large pile of photos of his slugging the homer off me on October 3.

"Hey, Ralph," he said, "good of you to help us out today."

"No problem, Bobby. I'm curious to see if anyone shows up."

Next thing I know, the promoter opens the door and outside I see a line of at least 300 guys waiting to get in. When they saw us, they broke into applause. They were filled with enthusiasm and even joy for a chance to see us together. God knows how many of those pictures they bought at five bucks a shot. And of course they wanted both our autographs—Bobby's alone wasn't good enough, and neither was mine. What's Abbott without Costello?

Afterward Bobby and I went out for a cup of coffee.

"Did you enjoy it, Ralph?" he said.

"I actually did, Bobby," I admitted. "We had a lot of satisfied customers."

"Would you ever think of doing it again?"

"Maybe. But considering the merchandise we sold, I think we were underpaid."

"Maybe you should negotiate the next deal, Ralph. I think you have a better business sense than I do."

"Well, it's got to be even-Steven between the two of us," I said.

"I wouldn't do it any other way. And I just want you to know that you'd be really helping me out."

Me helping out Bobby Thomson! What a strange concept . . . but one that came to pass.

I was able to negotiate our fee from $1,000 to $2,000, then $3,000, then $4,000, and finally $5,000 for a couple of hours a week. We did it several times a year over a number of years. My disdain for Bobby melted. I saw that he was a good guy with values not unlike mine. He loved his family, and his politics, like mine, were conservative. The chip on my shoulder finally fell off. I saw Bobby not as the perpetuator of the cheating scandal but as a foot soldier and not one of the generals who initiated the sign-stealing. And, in the aftermath of his home run, I began to understand that the hoopla had overwhelmed him. He was a shy man not cut out for media stardom. The hero business made him uncomfortable. Perhaps that was because he felt guilty about the cheating or perhaps because he simply didn't relish the spotlight.

The culmination of this partnership came in the months before the 50th anniversary of The Pitch in late 2000. Steiner Sports Marketing approached us. They wanted us to sign thousands of jerseys, pictures, bats, and balls. They were going all out with this Thomson-Branca coautographing phenomenon.

"How much do you think we can make from this?" asked Bobby when Steiner first approached us. "I wonder if he'd pay $30,000 or maybe $40,000 for the two of us?"

"Oh, I think he'll pay more than that, Bobby. Let me talk to the man."

We must have signed our names 20,000 times, but it was worth it. Dave Jurist and his son Anthony negotiated our deal. Steiner paid us *each* $220,000. But don't worry about Brandon Steiner; he made tons of money off this arrangement.

There's nothing like a mutually profitable transaction to seal a partnership. For my part, I felt that, for all the anguish that that October 3 had brought me, it also had made me some money. I felt comfortable with that, but it did not take away the fact that my Dodgers got cheated out of their rightful place in baseball history. The pain—the fact that the general public still didn't know the truth—could still keep me up at night. But I'd begun to come to peace with it, which is why I was taken aback when a reporter from the *Wall Street Journal* called me just about the time Bobby and I had cut our biggest deal.

January 31, 2001

ONTHS BEFORE THE article appeared that broke the scandal, its author, Josh Prager, got me on the phone. He wanted quotes; he wanted information; in short, he wanted to know what I knew and how I felt. I told him I had known about the sign-stealing since 1954 and had not talked about it since then and I was not going to talk about it now.

"Why?" he asked.

"Because I'm not going into it."

"Why not?"

"Because I've lived with it this long—and I can live with it longer. Besides, Bobby's become a friend."

"That doesn't mean you can't comment on what you think the Giants did during 1951," said Josh.

"What part of *no* don't you understand?" I said. "Whatever you learn, you're going to have to learn on your own."

Well, Prager did just that—and he learned plenty. He ran down the whole operation. He nailed down the facts; he came up with incontrovertible evidence; and he spelled it all out in black and white—the German telescope, the wiring, the buzzers, the July 19 date when Durocher announced the scheme to his players—it was all established and the huge impact it had on the Giants' turn-around in '51. Anyone reading the article could no longer think of the October 3 game or Bobby's home run in the same way again.

The next day I picked up the phone receiver and called Bobby. Remember—he and I, for the dozens of times we'd been together signing autographs, had never broached the issue.

"You read the article?" I asked Bobby.

"Sure," he said, "everyone's talking about it."

"What do you think?"

"I think, Ralph, that you must feel exonerated."

"I don't feel exonerated, but my tongue is definitely loosened."

The cat was out of the bag, and nothing or no one could stuff it back in. I relished the interviews that allowed me for the first time to say what I had been feeling.

We was robbed!

The interviews led me to express for the first time what my heart had been hungering to say for 50 years:

We was robbed!

Bobby was less happy about the interviews. He didn't want his glorious moment tainted. Who would? But the truth is the truth. For the most part, Bobby was truthful, but never went all the way. He admitted that he had received signs, but he claimed that in his final at-bat on October 3 he had not. I didn't believe him. Few did. Why, suddenly, with a chance to win the pennant, would a player ignore the system that got him into this very game? It made no sense.

Free to air my long-suppressed rage, I told one reporter that when you looked at the film of Bobby's swing, you saw him attacking the ball, like a lion attacking a wounded leopard. He knew what was coming.

The Thomson/Branca partnership was shaken. Bobby didn't like all this new attention to what had happened 50 years earlier, while I did. And I still do.

A Moment in Time

I N 2006, JOSH Prager, who had been researching the '51 scandal for years, published *The Echoing Green*, a detailed narrative history of exactly how the Giants did it. This engendered another round of stories and, at some point, Bobby said he was sick of me griping about what had happened. Well, if he was tired of my griping for a few months, imagine how I felt when, for more than 50 years, I bit my tongue. But Thomson and I kept in touch, and the bickering finally stopped.

Bobby was in assisted living in Georgia when he died in August 2010. I was genuinely saddened and accepted the invitation to attend his memorial service. He was a good man. And I proudly told everyone that, even though I had lost a game, I had made a friend.

Old-timers like to pontificate. An old-timer like me wouldn't let you put down this book without giving my view of baseball today.

Before I express my concerns, though, let me first express my gratitude. God has been good to me. He has given me a long life and, aside from my injuries, good health. I was blessed to be able to play in the big leagues. I was blessed to be a member of the Brooklyn Dodgers.

In 1999, when I traveled to Louisville to attend Pee Wee Reese's funeral, a flood of memories washed over me, many of the same memories that have populated this book. And in 2011, when Duke died, I was similarly transported back to that ballpark in Flatbush where, with the war over and the country booming, we met as young men and spent our summers in pursuit of a pennant. Pee Wee, Duke, Gilly, Furillo, Jackie, Campy and the pitching staff, Newcombe, Erskine, Roe, Loes, Labine, King, Barney, Banta, Podbielan, Rutherford, and on and on—these were men made of sterling. Win or lose, these were champions.

I recently called Oisk in Indiana, just to check in.

"Am I just being nostalgic, Carl, or am I right to say that no other team will ever have what we had in Brooklyn?"

"That's not being self-serving, Ralph. That's just being accurate. Think of the circumstances. Jackie, Campy, and Newk had just broken the color line. The fans practically lived at Ebbets Field. They felt more comfortable there than in their own apartments. That sort of intimacy was nothing short of amazing. It was actually a home that we shared with the people of Brooklyn. It was comfortable and familiar for everyone. It was all about hope and heart."

"Remember years later when people started talking about soul music, Oisk? Well, the Dodgers were the soul team. We played baseball with soul."

"Amen, brother."

Where is today's soul?

I'm not saying that today's players aren't good. There are dozens of marvelous players. Ethnic diversity has expanded the pool of talent and added excitement. The internationalization of America's major leagues is a great thing.

Salaries have risen to astronomical levels, and players are no longer the victims of exploitation—another great thing. The obsession with making megamillions, however, surely contributed to the widespread use of performance-enhancing drugs. After all was said and done, use of steroids was another form of cheating, not only giving unfair advantage to certain players but also breaking the hearts of the fans—especially the young ones—who presumed that the game was pure.

In spite of a retro trend to make new ballparks look old, many of them have the atmosphere of suburban shopping malls. The hypnotic glow of a giant high-def screen has you virtually glued to TV. Rather than watching live play with your own eyes, you're looking through the lens of a camera. The ear-shattering electronic sound effects and nonstop video gimmicks may be seen as entertainment, but they disrupt the essential pace of the game, which is relaxed, not flashy. Entertainment is the driving force behind the design and merchandising of modern baseball. As a result, the pure beauty of the game has been compromised.

Fundamentals are not taught as they once were. Players are out for themselves because of arbitration and the reliance on individual stats. Stimulated by a culture obsessed with celebrities, players hire all kinds of representation to make sure they get their share of media glory.

The old-timer can go on and on . . . but he won't.

I realize that the world changes. When I broke in, old-timers were saying that the forties were nothing like the golden days of the twenties and thirties. Old-timers have a tendency to bemoan the present and glorify the past. Old-timers are a proud lot. Part of me indulges in that and part of me fights it off. I've worked hard to stay current. I can work on my laptop and surf the Net. You can e-mail me and I can text you. At 85, I'm still out there explaining the greatness of insurance and, if you give me a few minutes, I'll convince you that a whole-life policy is still your best buy.

As we celebrate our 60th wedding anniversary, Ann and I look back at our lives with tremendous satisfaction. We enjoy a close and loving relationship with our beautiful daughters. We adore our grandsons Bobby Jr., Will, and Brian. I've been lucky to have a great father-son relationship with Bobby Valentine.

Through the years I've made it a regular practice to travel to Vero Beach and watch spring training. That's where I got close to Sandy Koufax. It's also where I inadvertently started an illustrious baseball career of the son of a friend who owned harness horses that raced in Florida. "My kid wants to be batboy for the Dodgers this winter," said my friend. "Can you arrange it, Ralph?" "Sure," I said. I got Tommy Lasorda to give the kid the job. That was in the early eighties. In 1998, at age 30, batboy Brian Cashman was named general manager of the New York Yankees.

The darkness of that day—October 3, 1951—has been overwhelmed by a life filled with light. Father Rowley was right when, after The Pitch, he said, "God chose you because He knew you'd be strong enough to bear this cross."

I thank God for that strength. I thank God for the energy and the time to finally tell my story. To be honest, on this final page, in spite of my abiding Catholic faith, I had planned to be true to the vindictive *paisan* within me and conclude with this thought: *In 1951, the Giants didn't win the pennant; the Giants stole the pennant.*

Now, though, I have some reservations. I'm feeling that I should strive for a higher sentiment. The better part of me wants to forgive the Giants and their scheme. Forgiving them is the right thing to do. I'm trying, but it looks like it's going to take me a couple of more years to get there.

Acknowledgments

THROUGH THE GOOD times, the bad times, and the in-between times, my wife, Ann, has always been there—and we have had some of each. Now as I grow older, she has become more solicitous than ever. Thank you, honey.

My daughters, Patti and Mary, have always loved their dad. They are loving, caring, beautiful, and so smart that I seek their advice all the time. They have given me smiles, laughs, happiness, support, and a grand slam of love.

Mom and Dad: Thanks for coming to America, meeting, marrying, and bringing me into this world. You taught the whole family the true values of life: love, respect, honesty, loyalty, integrity, and patriotism.

All my sisters were loving, kind, and very supportive: Antoinette (Nan) O'Connell, Annunziata (Nunce) Pisano, Anna DeLeonardis, Helen Algieri, Florence Saccone, Margaret Aquilino, and Rosemarie Leo.

My five brothers: Julius (Julie), Edward (Eddie), John, Paul, and Alfred (Al) were all loving and devoted. Julie was the prime reason we were so into baseball, as he played sandlot baseball when we were very young. He peaked our interest and then instructed us.

John was my closest friend and most devoted fan. He was my

coach. He was also a great father to his two sons, John G. and William "Billy," both very successful.

Which brings me to all my other nephews and nieces who were also successful in their endeavors and true Brancas. There are too many to mention all of them, but John and Jimmy O'Connell and Dr. Dan Pisano are worthy of a special note.

All my love: Bobby Valentine, my son-in-law; Bobby Valentine Jr., my grandson; William Barnes III, my grandson; Brian Barnes, my grandson; Tom Duffy; Thomas Gavin Duffy; Bob Lyons; Fay Vincent; Desmond O'Brien; Diarmaud Hogan; Peter Labatt; Leland Harris; Frank Casucci; Ernie Aloi; Nick Liapunov; Tony Veteri; Freddy Santore; Joe Pignatano; Tom Villante; George Ponte; Fred Viscogliosi; George Jimenez; Barry Winick; Ron Bennett; Sam Salvatore; Anthony Salvatore; John Brescia; Frank Merola; Eddie Poulson; William McCarthy; Andy Monte; Tom Turco; Dave Jurist; Anthony Jurist; Greg O'Brien; Joshua Prager; Joseph Salerno; Joseph Lamastro; Anthony "Moose" Muscato; Juan Couch; and David Ritz, my talented co-author. Thanks for a great job!

David Ritz would like to thank Ralph Branca, a wonderful man, for the privilege of cowriting his book. Gratitude to Brant Rumble, for superb editing; Nan Graham; David Vigliano; Bill Branca; John Branca; Andrew Muscato; my dad; my wife, Roberta; my daughters, Alison and Jessica; sons-in-law, Henry and Jim; grandkids, Charlotte, Ninz, James, and Isaac; sisters, Esther and Elizabeth; my fabulous nieces and nephews; loyal pals Harry Weinger, Herb Powell, Aaron Cohen, Dejon Mayes, James Austin, and Alan Eisenstock; the Tuesday morning God squad; and all friends of Bill W.

Jesus is my strength, my hope, and my joy.

Index

Index